Alexander Frederic Corbett

The climate and Resources of Upper India, and Suggestions for their Improvement

Alexander Frederic Corbett

The climate and Resources of Upper India, and Suggestions for their Improvement

ISBN/EAN: 9783337230210

Printed in Europe, USA, Canada, Australia, Japan

Cover: Foto ©Suzi / pixelio.de

More available books at **www.hansebooks.com**

THE
CLIMATE AND RESOURCES

OF

UPPER INDIA,

AND

SUGGESTIONS FOR THEIR IMPROVEMENT.

BY

A. F. CORBETT, Lieut.-Col.

Bengal Staff Corps.

LONDON:
W. H. ALLEN & CO., 13, WATERLOO PLACE.
1874.
[ALL RIGHTS RESERVED.]

PREFACE.

THIS book treats more particularly of the British possessions in Upper India, and is an attempt to show how the climate may be improved and the resources developed. If the suggestions here made are effectual in Upper India, they may also be of use in many other parts of the world where the climate is divided into dry and wet seasons, or which are liable to periods of drought.

A. F. CORBETT.

CLIMATE AND RESOURCES

OF

UPPER INDIA.

UPPER INDIA, or the Provinces under the Governments of the North-Western Provinces, the Punjab, and Oude, lies chiefly between the parallels of 25° and 33° of North Latitude, and between 70° and 80° of East Longitude, which limits it crosses diagonally from south-east to north-west.

The climate is divided into three well-defined seasons,—the rains, the cold weather, and the hot weather. The rains commence about the 15th or 20th of June, and last for about three months, till the 15th or 20th of September; commencing earlier and ending somewhat later in the south-eastern districts than in those more to the north-west. The temperature in the shade in the daytime during the rains may range from 85° to 90° or 95° Fahrenheit. The rainfall varies much in different localities; there is a greater precipitation about Benares and the eastern districts than the average, but the greatest occurs in the Teraee, or forest, at the foot of the Himalayas, and on the southern slopes of the Himalayas. The rainfall at Nynee Tal often exceeds one hundred inches in the year; and the rainfall at the foot of the hills under that station is about equal to, and sometimes exceeds, the rainfall at Nynee Tal. The annual average rainfall in the Dooab, or country between the Ganges and the Jumna, may be about twenty-four inches, a greater precipitation occurring in those districts nearer the hills. There is also a greater rainfall in Oude and Rohilcund, lying north of the Ganges, than in the Dooab. The least rainfall is about Mooltan, in the Punjab, where sometimes not more than five or six inches fall in the year.

For a month after the cessation of the rains the atmosphere is clear, and there is a bright hot sun, which quickly dries up much of the moisture left in the surface-soil, which was deposited in the rains.

About the commencement of November the cold weather may be considered to set in, when the plains of Upper India are favoured with about four months of clear, bracing weather, with often sharp frosts in the mornings, particularly pleasant and well suited to Europeans; but these frosts, which are more severe and frequent than formerly, are injurious to the country agriculturally; as various food-plants, particularly the arhar, are now more frequently killed by the frost than was formerly the case. The usual winds during the cold weather, *i.e.* from November to the end of February, are west, or from a few points north of west; and east winds are rare, except with a cloudy sky. It is generally said, the east winds in Upper India bring clouds; but it seems doubtful whether the clouds are the effect or the cause of the east winds. To this I will hereafter refer.

During the cold weather some rain generally falls, mostly in the months of December and January; the average cold-weather rainfall being from two to four or five inches, more usually falling in the Punjab, and to the west, than in the eastern parts of Upper India.

In the more southern parts the cold-weather crops sown in October and November are harvested; and in the more northern parts are ripening in the month of March. The winds then set in more steadily and with greater force from the west; and camp-life, enjoyable through the cold weather, begins to be unpleasant from heat and its accompanying wind and dust. This description of weather lasts, the wind steadily day by day increasing in force, throughout the month.

Towards the end of March the heat, wind, and dust have increased, and punkahs and tatties are required in the southern parts of Upper India, but are not generally in use in Rohilcund and further to the north-west till the middle or end of April, by which time we have the hot weather, or season of the hot winds, which lasts through May and June, till the commencement of the rains.

The utility of tatties, that is their cooling power, depends on the evaporation, caused by the hot dry winds, of water thrown on them; and as they are only used when the heat is unbearable without them, the hot weather, or season of the hot winds, may be considered well commenced from the time tatties are brought into use.

The chief characteristic of the hot winds is that they are westerly, that they mostly get up from about 8 to 10 A.M., some three or four hours after sunrise, when the surface of the country has become heated by the rays of the sun; they are at their greatest force about 2 or 3 P.M., after which they gradually decrease, as the direct incidence of solar heat on the surface of the country decreases, and generally die away about or shortly after sunset.

The nights during the season of the hot winds are generally calm, and it is not uncommon to have a slightly clouded sky and light east winds in the mornings. This, however, is more frequent in the more eastern parts, while further to the north-west the hot west wind sometimes continues through the night.

As Upper India lies between the parallels of 25° and 33° N., and the north-east trade-winds extend as far north as 30°, the prevalent winds to that degree of latitude should be east, and not west, were there not local causes at work acting adversely; and the winds north of the parallel of 30° should be more variable, and not so persistently from the west as they now are.

The fact of these hot west winds getting up daily shortly after sunrise, their period of greatest intensity being about 2 or 3 P.M., and their gradual decrease after that time till about sunset, when they die away, points to solar heat as the cause of their origin.

Solar heat is considered to be the primary cause of all winds, and we have merely to consider the causes which in Upper India tend to make the wind a west wind, and thus contrary to the direction of the trade-winds, in whose course Upper India lies.

We know that heated air expands and ascends, and its room is taken up by cooler, denser air, which rushes into its place to preserve an equilibrium, and to fill what would otherwise be a vacuum; or it may be that the cooler, denser air, by its greater specific gravity, sinks and spreads over the ground, forcing the lighter air to ascend. The result is the same,—a rush of air, *i.e.* a wind. The draught in an ordinary fire-place is caused by the expansion and ascension of the air over the fire as it becomes heated. The ascension is due to cooler, denser air sweeping along the floor, and displacing by its greater gravity the air over the fire as it becomes heated and is lighter. The histories of all large fires, from that of London to that of Chicago, state that there has been a wind during the time the fire was raging; but it is not always clear that there was a wind previous to the breaking out of the fire. The ascension of the heated air in these cases, or rather the rush of cooler denser air, to displace the lighter heated air, creates a large indraught, or, in other words, constitutes a wind.

The alternations of sea and land breezes which daily occur on the seashore, more particularly in tropical climates, and which moderate the heat of the climate, are an apt illustration of the influence of the sun in causing wind. As the land becomes heated with the rays of the sun, the air hanging over it becomes heated, and a rush of cooler air from the sea—the sea-breeze—takes place, which displaces the air heated by contact with the land, which rises. At night, on the contrary, as the land cools by radiation, the air in contact with it becomes cooler and heavier, and, by its greater specific gravity, sinks down to, and spreads over the sea, the water of which is not cooled by radiation to the same extent as the land, and displaces the warmer air resting on its surface. This is the land-breeze. The sea-breeze should, according to this theory, be stronger on the shore of a bare stony country, and the land-breeze stronger on the shore of a country well covered with vegetation. Whether such has, by observation, been found to be the case, I do not know.

The air of a country is not heated to any extent by the passage of the rays of solar heat through it, but by their coming in contact with the surface of the land, or objects on it. The air obtains its heat from contact with heated objects, the chief of which is the surface of the land; and is never so hot in the hottest days as the object from which it obtains its heat.

As the earth revolves on its axis, the eastern parts of a country are first presented to the influence of, and are heated by the rays of the sun. The air in contact with the soil will become heated and lighter, and cooler, denser air will, from its greater specific gravity, rush in and displace it, and cause it to ascend. As the land further to the west has been somewhat cooled down by radiation and the absence of solar heat during the night, and its superincumbent air has also become cooled, the air from that direction will, from its greater gravity, rush towards the east, and displace that which has become heated and is lighter; and thus we have west winds.

In a former paragraph, alluding to the general opinion that east winds in Upper India bring clouds, I said it seemed doubtful whether the clouds were the effect or the cause of the east winds. It appears to me highly probable that clouds caused by some meteorological disturbance having prevented the falling of the sun's rays on the soil, and hindered its becoming heated, have thus diminished the causes giving rise to the west winds, and we have, in consequence, a restoration of the normal north-east trade-winds. This seems the more probable, as, when a hailstorm or fall of rain occurs during the season of the hot winds, over a considerable tract of country, during the time the land is wet, and while there is great evaporation from the surface, we have east winds. In this case the vapour in the air, from evaporation, arrests the rays of the sun, and the surface is cooled by evaporation going on upon it. Thus it appears that while the causes producing the west winds, the chief of which I consider to be the heating of the surface, are in abeyance, the normal north-east trade-winds resume their sway. During the hot weather the thermometer often rises during the day to from 120° to 130° Fahrenheit in the shade, and all nature suffers. All woodwork exposed to the dry, hot air warps and splits, and speedily goes to rack and ruin.

It is generally acknowledged that the heat of Upper India has very much increased of late years, and various facts seem to show that such is the case. Early in the present century it was considered by the English residents in India unhealthy to use punkahs at night, and many did not do so. Now their use at night is universal.

It has been brought forward as a proof of a want of inventive faculty in our predecessors in India, that they were content with the hand punkah of the country which was in use amongst the natives, and did not invent the punkah now in use, which is suspended from the ceiling, for a number of years after we had obtained possession of the country. It appears to me that the suspended punkahs not being invented was probably owing to the fact that they were not required; the climate being cooler, the old hand punkahs were sufficient, and there was no urgent necessity for the suspended punkahs. As soon as the necessity arose, from increased heat of the climate, the suspended punkahs would be invented. Previous to their invention, punkahs could hardly have been used in bedrooms. Thermantidotes now in general use were not known fifty years ago. The first description we have of one was by Dr. Ranken, and was published with drawings in the Transactions of the Medical and Physical Society of Calcutta, in 1827. Punkahs were, I believe, first allowed in barracks for European troops in 1849, previous to which they were not considered necessary. I never used a punkah in my house before 1850 or 1851, and know many persons who did not use them at that time.

New barracks have been built throughout the country, mostly since 1857, giving much greater accommodation for the troops, and built on improved principles and better ventilated, built expressly for coolness; but they are described as unbearably hot, and now it is proposed to increase the number of hill stations, and keep as many of the European troops as possible in the hills. This is all very well as regards the infantry, but the cavalry and artillery cannot be kept in the hills. There are other Europeans too whose duties tie them to the plains, and who cannot get to the hills for the hot weather. All Government officials must keep to their posts, and so must Europeans in the employment of railways, &c.; for instance, the engine-drivers, whose duties perhaps require them to be more exposed than any other class of Europeans in India.

The new barracks are, as I said, unbearably hot; we cannot of course now say whether such buildings would have been so thirty or fifty years ago, when European troops lived in barracks of a very much inferior description, or what are now considered so; but there may be some of the old barracks in existence in which European troops formerly lived, and if they are now unfit for Europeans to live in, it is strong presumptive proof that the climate has become hotter and deteriorated.

Cooling apparatus is now being fitted to the railway carriages in Upper India, it being found that numerous deaths occurred from heat apoplexy, which the new appliances are to prevent. The cost of heat from an £. s. d. point of view, *i.e.* the amount of money annually spent in contrivances to mitigate it, must amount to a large sum, and is increasing.

The question of stationing more European troops in the hills has been more prominently brought forward as the climate has become hotter. They are to be sent to the hills to be away from the heat. The expense of providing accommodation for them in the hills will be great in the first instance, and the effects may be injurious in many ways to the country; and, after all, the British soldier in general prefers the plains, notwithstanding the drawbacks and inconveniences occasioned by the heat. I hope, however, to show how the heat of Upper India can be mitigated, and the climate so improved that there shall be no cause for removing the European troops from the plains, where they are more wanted. Supposing hill stations were made, it is as well to consider what would be the result of stationing a greater number of European troops in the hills. The sites of the stations will have to be cleared for barracks and parade-grounds, and the forests in their neighbourhood will be cut down as fuel: this will create greater surface-drainage.

The destruction caused by inundations in the valley of the Ardèche, the Po, and other European rivers, is attributed to increased surface-drainage, caused by cutting down the forests near their sources; and will not increased surface-drainage, caused by felling the forests in the Himalayas, lead to like disastrous consequences? The floods in the valley of the Sutlej, which carried away the railway bridge between Phillor and Loodianah, may probably be a result of cutting down the forests in the hills near the sources of this river, for timber for stations in the Punjab, &c.

In the hills, where the surface-soil is generally light vegetable soil formed of decomposed leaves, overlying rock, it is easily washed away; and any attempts to reclothe such precipitous hillsides with forest growth would be futile. It is, perhaps, enough to state here that Marsh, in his book "Man and Nature," gives instances where whole districts have been ruined and depopulated from the felling of forests on hillsides. Is it even possible that the forests on the hills in India can be cut down without similar results? Do we not see in hill stations in India landslips occurring in every direction, the result of cutting down the trees, or man's interference in some way with the natural surface and slope of the land? The case is different where tea or other plantations are formed, as here, if properly managed, attempts would be made to prevent loss of water by surface-drainage and washing away of the soil.

It is during the hot weather, the season of the hot winds, when we have this intense heat, that we hear of sunstroke and heat apoplexy.

Now sunstroke does not appear to be caused by the incidence of the direct rays of the sun alone, but by that combined with a high temperature of the surrounding air, as we find that during the hot weather, when Europeans cannot expose themselves to the sun without imminent danger of sunstroke in the plains, they can and do in the hills (where the direct rays of the sun are actually hotter, from the more rarefied state of the air, than in the plains) expose themselves and take violent exercise, play at cricket, &c., with perfect impunity, because the surrounding air is cooler.

Heat apoplexy appears to be suffocation from excessive heat. The cases of it mostly occur in the evening, often after sunset. It is hardly known in Southern India and Bengal, and is most prevalent in the hottest and driest parts of Upper India. Deaths from this cause are steadily increasing. The natives say it was almost unknown amongst them in Rohilcund some years ago, but now numerous deaths occur from it there. These deaths being due to great heat, the increased number of deaths from this cause may be taken as another circumstance showing that the heat of the climate has increased.

During the hot weather numbers of cattle die of starvation, finding hardly any herbage to eat, or are reduced to little more than skeletons, and feed chiefly on the leaves of trees, which they crop from the lower branches within their reach, or are broken from the higher branches, and thrown down to them by their attendants. The trees themselves suffer: their growth is arrested, the leaves wither and fall, and in a season hotter than usual the bark shrivels and cracks in all directions, from the intense heat and dryness of the air, as if scorched by fire, and the trees dry up and die.

This is no exaggerated picture. I saw numbers of trees of as much as one to two feet in diameter, which were killed in this way by heat, in 1868 and 1869, in the Budaon district, and many more trees which lost large branches, killed by the same cause. I have since then seen more trees killed by the dry heat, but 1868 was the first year in which I noticed it, and it was talked of amongst the natives as something previously unknown in Rohilcund.

The damage done in this way is increased by the wind, which, by bringing fresh particles of dry air continuously into contact with the leaves, causes greater evaporation from them; and we see its effects in the more drooping and withered appearance of the leaves of trees and vegetables in the evening of a windy day than in the evening of a still day.

The manner in which hot dry air kills trees is plain. When the daily evaporation of moisture from the leaves exceeds the amount of moisture a tree can daily take up by its roots, the tree must wither and die. This is merely a case of daily expenditure exceeding daily income, when the principal has to be encroached on, and bankruptcy occurs,— the principal in the case of a tree being its normal amount of sap. It depends, then, on the amount of moisture in the ground within reach of the roots of a tree, and the capability of the roots for pumping it up, whether the tree will suffer or not from evaporation caused by a dry, hot air. In the cases of the trees killed by heat in the Budaon district in 1868 and 1869, it is remarkable that the trees so killed were mostly on low-lying lands, and invariably on land with a hardened surface-soil. On the higher land, with a loose, sandy surface-soil, I saw no trees killed by the heat. If we dig into these soils, we soon discover the reason. Beneath the land with the hardened, compacted soil we find next to no moisture, while beneath the loose, sandy surface-soil we meet with a much larger amount of moisture present in the subsoil.

Heat and moisture are necessary for vegetation; and we find that the most luxuriant and rank vegetation occurs in those parts of the world where great heat and moisture are combined. But where there is heat without moisture, or rather with a minimum amount of moisture, as in the Sahara and other deserts, no vegetation, or next to none, exists, or can exist. The dry heat of these deserts, and of Upper India during the hot season, very much exceeds that of any country where there is a great amount of vegetation. Of two countries lying under the same degree of latitude, the one well covered with forests and vegetation, and the other devoid of vegetation, the summer heat of the latter will greatly exceed that of the former. The heat of the plain of the Amazon river—a country covered with forests—is said to be sometimes as high as 106° Fahrenheit in the shade, on the equator, for two hours in the day, from 2 till 4 P.M., when the sun is near the line. This is considered the greatest heat known in a forest-covered country, with consequently a damp climate; and here, also, is the richest, or rather rankest vegetable growth in the world, the result of great heat and moisture combined.

Other conditions being equal, a difference of ·9 of a degree of heat, Fahrenheit, is considered the allowance that should be made between any two places for every degree of latitude difference there may be in their geographical positions, in computing their mean temperature. Then, as Upper India lies between the parallels of 25° and 33° N., its mean temperature, according to its geographical position, should be from 22·5 to 29·7 Fahrenheit lower than places on the equator; instead of which, if we examine a climatological chart, giving the isothermal lines, we find the line of greatest mean heat runs through Upper India; and only in Upper India and in Africa does the line run to the north of the tropic of Cancer.

In Africa the cause is the Sahara. In Upper India the whole country, during April, May, and June, is virtually a desert; and it is the great heat generated by it during these months which causes the line of greatest mean heat to recede so far from the equator.

The excessive heat of the plains of Upper India is, then, not due to their geographical position, but is in opposition to the laws of nature as regards the effect of latitude on climate; and I will endeavour to point out to what circumstances this great heat may be attributed.* Firstly, the excessive heat is due to bare plains, the surfaces of which becoming heated, heat the air coming in contact with them; and this effect is intensified by the hardened condition of the surface-soil, which does not absorb and radiate heat, but reflects or retains it, as rock or stone would. Secondly, it is caused by surface-drainage, which facilitates the running-off of the rainfall, and prevents its penetrating the soil.

The bare plains are of two descriptions,—the uncultivated and the cultivated. The former are bare throughout the year, except in the rains, when they may have a little grass on them. As I shall more fully describe these uncultivated lands (which, by the bye, are often called unculturable lands) when I point out the causes to which they are due, I shall say no more about them at present than that they are spread over the whole country; their extent and positions are laid down in the Revenue Survey maps; they are attached to different villages—in fact, there is hardly a village which does not possess some uncultivated land; and these uncultivated lands are not assessed for revenue to Government. As, however, they produce some grass in the rains, it may be to the interest of the zemindars, when these lands have become impoverished and only produce poor crops, to allow them to remain uncultivated, in that case paying no revenue, to keeping them cultivated and paying some revenue on them.

* *See* Appendix A, p. 101.

The cultivated lands are mainly under two descriptions of crops,—the rain crops and the cold-weather crops.

The rain crops, sown shortly after the commencement of the rains, are reaped in October and November. The lands occupied by them are then left untouched by the plough till the next rains, except such fields as may be required for sugar-cane, which is planted in February or March. Should, however, there be more copious falls of rain than usual in the cold weather, advantage is sometimes taken of the softened state of the soil to plough up some of these rain-crop fields by landlords who cultivate some of their own land, and by tenants whose tenure insures their having the land for the following year; but not by ordinary tenants, who hold from year to year, know not how long they may keep the land, and who rarely hold the same fields two years running, but are moved from field to field at the will of the landlord or his agent, or at their own request.

The natives are well aware of the benefits of breaking up the soil in the cold weather, to expose it to the ameliorating influences of air, heat, and rain; but only a few of them are in a condition to avail themselves of it. However, broken up, or not broken up, with the exception of the land planted with sugar-cane, indigo, or some such crop, the land which has borne a rain crop one year remains a bare plain throughout the succeeding cold and hot weather. When broken up, the physical condition of the surface-soil only is altered, and it is rendered capable of absorbing and radiating heat; but its powers of absorbing and radiating heat are limited by the shallowness of the ploughing. Still this has some effect, as the temperature of a hot weather succeeding a cold weather, in which more than the usual amount of rain has fallen, and more land has been broken up, is noticeably cooler than after a cold season in which less rain has fallen, and less ground has been broken up.

The cold-weather crops are sown in October and November, and are reaped in March and April. The bulk of these crops consists of wheat, barley, and gram (*Cicer arietinum*). After these crops are reaped, the fields are left untouched by the plough till the rains, unless wanted for indigo, when it is slightly scratched with hoes, the seed sprinkled on the surface, and forced into growth by irrigation. Sometimes the hoeing of the ground even is not considered necessary, and the surface is prepared for the seed by dragging a branch of a tree over it. This shows the extent to which the natives trust to irrigation. Where water is to be had they trust to it, and it alone, for a crop, and neglect all other precautions,—such as preparing a proper bed for the seed, manuring, &c.

With the exception of what small amount of land is sown with indigo, the land occupied by the cold-weather crops is a bare plain during the hot weather, the months of April, May, and June, the time of greatest heat. Thus the whole of the uncultivated land not covered with jungle, and the whole of the cultivated land, with but trifling exceptions, are during the hottest time of the year bare plains; and it is well known that wherever on the face of the earth, in tropical or subtropical regions, large bare plains occur, the heat is much more intense than where, in the same latitudes, we find countries covered with forest growth. For instance, the Sahara, the deserts of Arabia and Persia, and the plains of Upper India, are notorious as being the hottest places in the world; and the heat of these places is universally allowed to be the result of the incidence of the rays of solar heat on bare plains. The heat is intensified by the hardened condition of the surface-soil, which does not absorb and radiate heat, but retains or reflects it, as rock or stone would. The power of reflecting heat possessed by any object is in inverse ratio to its power of absorption and radiation. The action of heat in this particular seems to be almost identical with that of light. The rougher the surface of any object, and the more irregularities it possesses, the greater is its power of absorption and radiation of heat, and the less its power of reflection. On the other hand, the smoother and harder the surface of any object, the greater is its power of reflection, and the less its power of absorption and radiation.

Again, the power of retaining heat possessed by any object is also in inverse ratio to its power of absorption and radiation; thus rocks and hardened baked earth, which require some length of time to become thoroughly heated, from the great amount of heat thrown off their surfaces by reflection, when heated, require also a long time to cool down again. The terms length of time and long time here used are merely comparative, and are used as contrasted with the time required by loose porous bodies to become heated or cool down again.

If we were to take two ordinary paving-flags of equal density and similar composition, and reduce one to powder and leave the other whole, and spread the powder resulting from pulverization over the same extent of surface it occupied before being reduced to powder, we should find that its power of *reflecting* and *retaining* heat had been decreased, and its power of *absorbing* and *radiating* heat had been increased; and we should have a standard to compare it with in the flag left unbroken.

The above experiment will show the difference that takes place in the absorptive and radiative powers, and consequently in the powers of reflecting and retaining heat, by reducing a stone to powder, that is by changing its density; but I have said the stones should be of similar composition, as different stones and soils have very different powers of absorption and radiation, which must not be overlooked.

Marsh, in his book "Man and Nature," in a note on page

144, says,—"Composition, texture, and colour of soil are important elements to be considered in estimating the effects of the removal of the forest upon its thermoscopic action." "Experience has proved," says Becquerel, "that when the soil is bared it becomes more or less heated (by the rays of the sun), according to the nature and colour of the particles which compose it, and according to its humidity, and that in the refrigeration resulting from radiation we must take into account the conducting power of those particles also. Other things being equal, silicious and calcareous sands, compared in equal volumes with different argillaceous earths, with calcareous powder or dust, with humus, with arable and with garden earth, are the soils which least conduct heat. It is for this reason that sandy ground, in summer, maintains a high temperature even during the night. We may hence conclude that when a sandy soil is stripped of wood the local temperature will be raised. After the sands follow successively argillaceous, arable, and garden ground, then humus, which occupies the lowest rank. If we represent the power of calcareous sand to retain heat by 100, we have, according to Schubler,

For (silicious?) sand	95·6
,, arable calcareous soil	74·3
,, argillaceous earth	68·4
,, garden earth	64·8
,, humus	49·0

"The retentive power of humus, then, is but half as great as that of calcareous sand. We will add that the power of retaining heat is proportional to the density. It has also a relation to the magnitude of the particles. It is for this reason that ground covered with silicious pebbles cools more slowly than silicious sand, and that pebbly soils are best suited to the cultivation of the vine, because they advance the ripening of the grape more rapidly than chalky and clayey earths, which cool quickly. Hence we see that in examining the calorific effects of clearing forests, it is important to take into account the properties of the soil laid bare."—Becquerel, " Des Climats et des Sols boisés," p. 137.

In India the heating of loose sandy soil in the day and its cooling during the night, can hardly have escaped the notice of any one who has walked over it. Its coolness in the morning compared with that of the neighbouring fields of a more clayey character of soil with a hardened surface, is remarkable, and is due to its radiative power, caused by the loosened state of division of its particles. The loose sandy soils are in the morning often wet with dew, when there is no dew on the hardened surface of the fields close by, showing that the surface temperature of the former has been reduced below dew-point, while it has not been reduced to that extent on the latter soils.

Were the soil of the fields with the hardened surface broken up and pulverized, it being of a more clayey nature, a better radiator, and not so retentive of heat, its temperature would be reduced below that of the sandy soil, and it would condense a greater amount of dew on its surface. Again, the power of retaining heat possessed by humus being less than that of purely mineral soils, the greater the amount of humus incorporated with the soils of our fields, the greater would be their powers of absorbing and radiating heat, and the greater the influence they would exert in reducing the temperature of a hot climate ;—a strong reason for burying as much vegetable matter as possible in the soil.

If we reverse the experiment of the paving-stones and take ordinary earth, and by moistening it and using pressure bring it into a state as nearly as possible resembling stone, we shall find that we have increased its reflective and retentive properties, and reduced its powers of absorption and radiation. This operation is performed every day in brickmaking. We have only to compare the reflective and retentive powers of sun-dried bricks with those of the loose earth from which they were made, and we shall find they have increased in proportion to the increased density of the materials composing them and the smoothness of their surfaces, and have lost in the same proportion their powers of absorption and radiation.

Irrigation is a somewhat analogous operation. By it the whole surface-soil is brought into the condition of sun-dried bricks; the more water that has been applied to the land the harder the soil becomes, and while its powers of absorption and radiation are reduced, those of reflection and retention of heat are increased; and we also find that the power of capillary attraction possessed by the land is increased, and that the soil so compacted will sooner become dried up than soil left loose and open, partly from the fact of the interstices between its particles having been reduced in size, thus increasing its capillarity, and partly from the increased heat of the surface. Notwithstanding this, the advocates of irrigation, while allowing that the heat of Upper India has increased of late years, deny that irrigation has had anything to do with causing the increased heat. I do not know how they can set aside these ordinary laws of nature,—perhaps they may be able to explain how it is to be done.

The soil of every field becomes somewhat caked on the surface during the growth of a crop on it, from the effects of any rain, or the dew which may drop from the crop upon it, and becomes hardened and dries up, from the combined effects of direct evaporation from the surface of the soil and the secondary effects of the evaporation from the leaves of the crop of the moisture which it had taken up by its roots.

The greater the amount of rainfall there has been during the period of the growth of the crop, provided there have also been some periods of dry, hot, sunshiny weather, the more will the soil be caked and hardened, and the greater will be its power of reflecting heat and the less its power of absorption and radiation. This increased power of reflecting heat, and decreased power of absorbing and radiating it, are brought to a high state of perfection, and are fully developed in irrigated lands, particularly in those irrigated from canals with an unlimited supply of water; for here, as in the case of rain, the greater the amount of water supplied to the land the more will the land become hard and consolidated. I will, as an example, take a field of wheat. The land is prepared by being ploughed and reploughed, or rather scarified some two or three inches deep about ten or twelve times during the rains, and immediately after they have ceased. Perhaps not so often on canal-irrigated lands as on lands not so irrigated. The object of these frequent ploughings or scarifyings is said to be to bring all grass and other vegetable matter there may be in the soil to the surface, where it is collected and often burnt, thus further diminishing the amount of vegetable matter in the soil. The seed is sown in the latter part of October, and in a few days, when the blades show above ground, the field is irrigated; the surface-soil is converted into loose mud, which, on drying, forms a crust; this crust cracks in all directions from the heat of the sun; the water, which had thoroughly soaked the loosened surface-soil and only slightly moistened the upper part of the hard *pan* below it, is dried up in a few days. Having mentioned the pan, it will be as well to describe it before proceeding further.

The pan is formed by the treading of men and cattle, and in England the pressure of the sole of the plough has something to do with its formation; not, however, in India, where there is no flat sole to the plough, and the implement itself is very light. In ploughing a piece of ground, drawing the furrows six inches apart, the bullocks taking steps of two feet, and two bullocks yoked to the plough, as is universally the case in Upper India, there will be four footprints on every square foot of ground every time the land is ploughed. This is only taking into calculation the footprints of the cattle in ploughing. This repeated every time the land is ploughed, some ten or twelve times a year, and having gone on for ages, must have consolidated the soil below the loosened arable surface-soil, the more so as advantage is always taken of a wet state of the soil for ploughing the land.

When it is required in India to make the bed of a tank watertight, it is recommended to keep it wet and turn buffaloes into it, as their treading effectually puddles the bed of the tank and prevents water being lost through it by percolation. In the same way that the treading of the bed of a tank by buffaloes prevents escape of water, so does the treading of cattle prevent water falling on the surface sinking to the subsoil. The existence of the pan is doubted by some persons, who consider it a myth, but its reality, and its greater density, compared with the subsoil below it, are easily proved by testing it with water, and watching how long it requires to disappear by absorption in the soil.

I tried with a tin tube three or four inches in diameter. First, I had two or three inches of the surface-soil of a field (the soil annually disturbed by the plough) scraped off I pressed the tube firmly on, or rather in, the soil, and poured into it a certain amount of water. I tried again, removing twelve and fifteen inches of the soil. This experiment was repeated a number of times, and invariably with the same result; the water was more quickly absorbed where I had a greater depth of soil removed, than when only the surface-soil disturbed by cultivation was removed; thus demonstrating the greater density and impermeability to water of the soil immediately below the loosened arable soil, compared with the soil at a greater depth, which is not to so great an extent affected by the treading of cattle on the surface. The more consolidated soil constitutes the *pan*; its greatest density is immediately below the soil broken up mechanically in cultivation, and it gradually decreases in density until it becomes undistinguishable from the natural condition of the soil below it.

To return to our wheat field. Water is again turned on, the loose surface-soil is converted into a liquid mud, and is carried by gravitation and deposited in the fissures made by the heat on drying up, after it had on the previous occasion been irrigated. This process is repeated time after time, until every pore of the soil is plugged up, and the land becomes almost hermetically sealed. In this state of the soil healthy action is impossible.

The crop is reaped in March or April, when the surface-soil presents a smooth glazed appearance, in the very best possible physical condition for retaining and reflecting heat; and in the very worst possible physical condition for absorbing and radiating heat. In fact, we have brought the soil into a condition as much resembling stone as possible, and in this state it remains during the hottest months of the year, increasing the intensity of the heat, until the rains commence.

The consequence of this is, that when the soil has become heated by the sun during the day it cannot part with its heat at night by radiation, as a loosened soil would; the following day the rays of the sun fall on a still warm surface, instead of a surface chilled by radiation, and less solar heat is required to raise its temperature, and eventually the temperature of the atmosphere, to a degree obnoxious both to animal and vegetable life.

The daily work of the sun, in the case of a country with a hardened reflecting surface-soil, is confined to raising the temperature of an already warm surface. No depth of soil is heated, the whole energy of the sun's heat is expended on the surface skin-deep.

On the other hand, when the soil is deeply broken up and well pulverized—the mass of soil so broken up loses at night, by radiation to the depth it has been broken up and pulverized, the heat it acquired by absorption the previous day,—the rays of the sun fall in the morning on a surface chilled by radiation, and probably wet with dew, below which is a mass of soil also chilled by radiation. The daily work of the sun, in this case, is first to convert the dew deposited on the surface (should dew have formed) into vapour, and afterwards to raise the temperature of the mass of the soil as deeply as it was pulverized and has been chilled by radiation.

A large amount of the heat of the sun will be expended in converting the dew into vapour, and a further amount in raising and keeping up the temperature of the mass of loosened soil. The amount of heat that will make a reflective surface unbearably hot will have but a slight effect in raising the temperature of an absorbent surface, particularly when backed up by absorbent substances; and here we have an absorbent surface backed up by a mass of absorbent soil. The heat of the climate of a country being obtained from and dependent on the heat of the surface of the country, the more we reduce the heat of the surface the more must the climate of a country be reduced in temperature.

The following experiments show the difference between the absorbent powers of a pulverized soil and one left hard and compact.

On the 12th April, 1871, I found, at four P.M., in a field which had been twice irrigated for the cold-weather crop, that the thermometer, held two feet above the ground, stood at 100° Fahrenheit, shaded. On the surface of the ground, also shaded, it stood at 111°; and when a hole was dug ten inches or a foot deep, the thermometer placed in it, and covered with an inch of the loosened soil, it went down in less than ten minutes to 82°.

This was an imperfect experiment, because I could not keep away the external heat whilst the soil was being dug and broken up, still it showed a difference of 29° Fahrenheit between the temperature of the surface and of the soil some ten inches or at the most a foot below it. I had the hole, which was about two feet in diameter, filled up with the soil I had taken from it, and on the 30th April, at four P.M., I made further trials in the same field.

On the surface of the field, and within three or four yards of where I had made the former trial, I found the thermometer, shaded, stood at 108°; and when the soil was dug up and tried as before, at about ten inches deep, it was 90°. This only gave a difference of 18°, much less than in the former trial, which I account for from the fact of numbers of men and cattle having passed over it, it being between the village and the threshing-floor, and by their passing and repassing had broken up the smooth surface. At the same time I also tested the surface, and also the soil ten inches deep of the hole I made and had filled up on the 12th April, and here, within three or four yards of the place where the last experiment was made, the thermometer, shaded, but exposed to external air, showed 102° on the loosened surface, and also 102° ten inches below it.

In the first case, where the surface was smooth and unbroken, the difference between heat of surface and soil ten inches or a foot below it was 29°. In the second case, where the surface had been broken by men and cattle walking over it, the difference was reduced to 18°, showing the increased absorbent power from the surface having been broken into a layer of dust. In the third case there was no difference between the heat on the surface and the heat ten inches or a foot below it, *but the heat of the surface was 6° lower than that of the surrounding ground,* although the hole was only about two feet in diameter, and the heat of its surface must have been greatly affected and raised by the surface heat of the land around it. Still, under these adverse circumstances, there was a reduced temperature of 6°. Were the surface of any large extent of country broken up and pulverized, the reduction in its surface temperature would, doubtless, be much greater, and the temperature of the atmosphere, which obtains its heat, by contact from the surface of the earth, and is never so hot in the daytime as the surface of the earth, would also be proportionately reduced.

In other trials I made I found the temperature at ten inches or a foot below the surface, where it was hard and unbroken, was always from 80° to 84°, but where broken, it more closely approximated to the heat of the surface, which was invariably below that of the surrounding unbroken land. This was the case at all hours of the day; and in the mornings the surface temperature of the broken-up soil was much below that of the unbroken surface close by, as was also the mass of soil to the depth it had been loosened.

The experiments I made were on fields irrigated only two or three times during the season, from wells where the water is only scantily supplied; had they been carried out on lands irrigated by canals, where the water is more frequently supplied and in greater quantity, the difference in temperature between surface and subsoil would probably have been greater in the case of fields with an unbroken surface-soil.

There is, however, another cause of the hardened condition of the soil, which, as it affects, perhaps, more than anything else the agricultural prosperity of the country, must not be overlooked, and that is, the deficiency of vegetable matter in it. It is this want of vegetable matter which allows the soil to bind into a compact mass, prevents its aëration, and renders deep cultivation more difficult.

This want of vegetable matter in the soil is caused by the stubble of the cereals and cold weather crops being eaten down as close as possible to the ground, the leaves of trees and stubble of the thicker-stemmed crops, and the woody stems of cotton and other plants, being carried off and used as fuel, as also is all cattle-dung, which is carefully collected and dried for that purpose, except during the rains; and any small remains of vegetable matters there may be on the land are carried away by surface-drainage.

The country plough, too, it must be noted, has no mould-board, and does not invert the surface-soil, it merely scratches it (it is not a plough, properly speaking, but merely a pointed implement which is drawn through the soil), and does not bury in the soil what manurial matters there may be on the surface; these may in the act of ploughing become mixed with the soil to some extent, but being of less specific gravity than the mineral soil, much is left on the surface, and is liable to be washed away.

It is common to hear complaints of a want of manure, and to see statements in the Indian papers to the effect that no improvement can take place in the agriculture of Upper India as long as cattle-dung is used as fuel, implying that cattle-dung is the sole or chief manure, for which there is no substitute.

The statement, however, is only partially correct. Cattle-dung, it is true, contains all the elements of fertility required by crops, and by using it as fuel all its organic, vegetable, or volatile constituents, are lost for the time, and only its mineral or non-volatile constituents remain available as manure.

Cattle-dung acts beneficially in two ways. Firstly, by supplying the manurial substances required and taken up by crops during their growth; and secondly, by improving the physical texture or condition of the soil, by which is meant its permeability to air and water. The loss by burning, as before stated, is the organic, vegetable, or volatile matter—its woody, and vegetable fibre and tissue—which, by incorporation with the soil, would have improved its physical texture or condition, have made it more open and porous, and more pervious to air and water, from which it would have had an increased power of abstracting fertilizing matters.

Liebig held the opinion that as long as the ashes of plants were returned to the soil, there was no necessity for returning to the soil the organic or volatile parts, *provided the physical condition of the soil were perfect.*

When a soil is rich in the mineral ingredients required by crops, it is probable that improving the texture of the soil by breaking it up deeply will be of more immediate benefit to the crops grown on it than an application of manure combined with shallow cultivation, and this deep cultivation of the soil might cause increased crops for years, but eventually a diminution of fertility would ensue from the abstraction from the soil of the mineral food of plants. What is really required is a combination of deep cultivation and the use of manure. Dung is now epigrammatically described as *food minus growth.* Food gains nothing by passing through the body of an animal; on the contrary, it passes through a course of fermentation, during which it undergoes a loss to the extent of its constituents taken up for the formation of the structure and increase of the body, and to make up for daily waste of tissue, and to maintain animal heat in the case of young growing animals. In the case of grown-up animals the former causes are wanting, and the food only suffers a loss of such materials as are required to make good daily waste of tissue and to keep up animal heat. According to this view of the case, the dung of grown-up animals should be of greater manurial value than that of young animals, as less is abstracted from it; and such in practice is found to be the case.

Again, dung being "food minus growth," the quality of the dung of an animal, as a manure, is dependent in a great measure on the quality of the food supplied to it. The stomach of an animal will only abstract from the food sufficient to make good daily waste (except in the case of growing or fattening animals), and should the food be rich in the constituents required for assimilation by the animal economy, the excess will be rejected, and pass through the animal unassimilated. On the contrary, should the food be poor in the constituents required for assimilation, the percentage of those constituents abstracted from it would be greater than it would be in the case of a richer food, and the balance remaining would be proportionately less. The constituents of the food, taken up by animals for the nourishment of their bodies are those of the greatest manurial value, and when an animal exists on food from which it can barely abstract sufficient nutriment to support life, its dung will be of the least possible value as a manure, properly so called; still the vegetable fibre and tissue composing it will be valuable, as supplying a mechanical means of improving the physical condition of the soil.

The cattle in Upper India are driven out in the mornings to pick up what few blades of grass and leaves of trees they can, and on returning home in the evenings, some of them may get a small supply of chopped or broken-up straw; their food during the drier part of the year, from January till

June, besides being limited in quantity is deficient in quality; and the volatile parts of their dung being almost void of ammoniacal ingredients, can be of but little value as a manure except so far as they would improve the texture of the soil and make it pervious to air and water. But as dung, after all, is only food minus growth, if we apply the food of animals to the soil as a manure, instead of using it as a food, we should obtain greater results, as we should be using the whole food, instead of food minus growth, that is, the whole, instead of a part, as manure. This system is known as green manuring. It may appear a waste of food to grow a crop to bury in the soil, simply as a manure for a crop which is to succeed it; and so, no doubt, it is, in cold and temperate climates, where only one crop can be grown in a year; but the case is different in countries like Upper India, where we can grow tall crops as jowar (*Holcus sorghum*), and other rain-plants, some five or six feet high, in two or two and a half months from the time of sowing, and bury them in the ground before the end of the rainy season, at a time of the year when there is no want of food for cattle. A good crop of jowar, of two or two and a half months' growth, may weigh from 50 to 100 tons per acre, so we can in this way supply that amount of manure to the land. This manure is on the spot, and there is no expense of carriage. Supposing 80 per cent. of the crop to be water, it leaves in the one case ten, and in the other twenty, tons of vegetable matters as manure, after deducting the water or sap of the plants, which, however, is useful in promoting fermentation, as also in adding so much moisture to be buried in the soil.

It is not necessary that the crop grown to bury in the soil should be one that might have been used for cattle-food. All vegetable matters act as manures to the soil; and if other crops can be grown more economically or conveniently than those which might have furnished cattle-food, by all means let them be grown.

In the case of farmyard manure, composed chiefly as it is of cattle-dung and straw, the materials for making it have first to be carried from the field to the homestead, and then back to the field, when wanted as a manure; and after all it is only the balance of the food or crop: it has been reduced both in quantity and quality, and still its bulk and weight are the chief obstacles to its use, as it will not repay the cost of its carriage to any distance. Farmyard manure, too, in England, generally contains about 70 or 80 per cent. of water. By green manuring all this carriage is saved, the bulk and manurial properties of the crop are not in any way impaired or reduced, and when the crop is buried in the soil the gases arising from its fermentation and decomposition enrich the soil which arrests them; and at the same time the gases, by their chemical action, and the vegetable fibre and tissue (which gradually decomposes and becomes humus) mechanically prevent the soil binding into a hard, unyielding mass.

The only expense of green manuring is the seed required for the crop which it is intended to use as a manure. Green manuring is seldom practised in temperate climates, because of the time that would be lost in growing a crop for manure. Not having green manuring to rely on, greater care is taken of farmyard manure, as a means of enriching the land, and to keep it open and porous. This latter object has also been effected by subsoil drainage.

The Chinese are said to practise green manuring to a great extent, and to grow heavy crops of clover merely to bury as a manure. As the Chinese are considered amongst the best agriculturists in the world, a lesson might be taken from them on this point, as regards a system of agriculture suited to the climate and requirements of Upper India.

The heat and aridity of the climate of Upper India, so far as they are due to bare plains and the hardness of the soil of the country, will diminish in proportion to the increase of forests and vegetation, and deeper cultivation and loosening of the soil; or, in other words, the heat arising from the non-absorptive and non-radiative state of the surface of the country will not be produced and cannot exist when it is made absorptive and radiative. The second cause of the excessive heat and aridity of the hot weather of the plains of Upper India is surface-drainage; and surface-drainage is due to two sets of causes, the one natural and the other artificial.

The natural causes of surface-drainage, such as the gradual formation of streams and valleys and the wearing away or degradation of the surface by the action of rain, are laid down in any standard work on physical geography or geology, and these may be passed over with the remark that in former days, when the population of any country was scanty, and when more land remained covered with forest growth, and less land had been brought under cultivation, more of the rainfall would have been arrested by the earth and less would have found its way by surface-drainage to the streams and rivers, which probably in those days were confined in well-defined channels, and were amply capacious to convey to the sea the amount of water which found its way to them without flooding the land near them. Forests and woods preserve moisture in a country in so far as they prevent or retard surface-drainage by their leaves, which fall and form a soft porous carpet on the surface; this yearly increasing in depth holds water like a sponge, the lower layers gradually rot and become incorporated with the soil; thus, in the course of time, there is in every forest (where not carried away by surface-drainage), above the mineral soil a layer of loose humus, the remains of decayed leaves, on which are other layers of leaves in varying stages of decay, the whole forming a mass which freely admits water, and prevents its escape by surface-drainage. The shade of the trees prevents the incidence of the direct rays of the sun; and the trees break the force of the wind and prevent the surface of the ground being swept and dried by them.

Thus forests preserve moisture in a country, firstly, by their soil being in a condition to arrest and retain water; and secondly, by the trees preventing the incidence of the sun's rays on the surface, and checking the force of the winds; thus the two chief causes of evaporation are absent. Some slight amount of water is evaporated from the surface, but the greater part gradually sinks into the subsoil, whence it is taken up by the roots of trees, to be again given off by their leaves in vapour, or finds its way by percolation, nature's own system of subsoil drainage, to the nearest watercourses. The ground under thick forests, where the leaves have been allowed to accumulate and decay on the surface, is always moist, showing that the amount of water lost by evaporation from the leaves of the trees and the surface of the ground does not equal the amount of yearly precipitation, and, in consequence, we find that springs and watercourses often originate in wooded lands and convey away some of the surplus water. This seems to have been the state which existed in most countries before the wants of an increasing population led to a clearance of forests for agricultural purposes.

The artificial causes of surface-drainage must have been prominently called into play from the time that man commenced to till the earth, as every operation of husbandry, by loosening and exposing the surface of the soil to the action of the sun, the wind, and the rain, would diminish the cohesion of its particles, and bring it into a state more readily acted on by them.

The more remote artificial causes have been at work for such ages, and their results have become so extensive, that they are generally regarded as natural causes, and it is not uncommon to hear the terms natural drainage and surface-drainage used as if synonymous, showing that all surface-drainage has now come to be considered as natural drainage. The more remote causes of surface-drainage are so spread throughout the country, and are so extensive, that any attempt to grapple with them would be futile at present. It will be time to look after them when the more immediate causes of surface-drainage have been modified. The more immediate causes of surface-drainage are numerous and must be separately considered.

Roads are one great cause of surface-drainage. They act in this way. The ordinary unmetalled road soon gets worn into ruts by the action of cart wheels, or men or cattle passing over it. In the dry weather the loose dust is blown away from the roads, and their level is lowered, the rain falling on the land on the sides of the roads finds its way to them, and they become the drainage channels of the country. In some cases attempts are made to rectify this by digging continuous drains on both sides of the roads, and throwing the soil dug from them on the roads to raise them. The rain then falling on the road and on the land on both sides of the road, finds an exit by the ditches, and they instead of the roads become the drainage channels of the country. Eventually both the road and the land on its sides are washed away and become ravines, these spread, eating back their way into the surrounding country, which thus becomes useless for cultivation. The metalled roads are generally somewhat raised above the level of the country, the soil to raise them being taken from continuous drains by their sides, which, as in the case of the unmetalled roads, become the drainage channels of the country by which the land on both sides bordering the roads gets carried away. This might be prevented by making ridges of earth on the sides of the land or fields abutting the roads, and, instead of continuous ditches acting as drains by the roads, having separate pits or tanks to arrest the flow of the water, which would be limited to what fell on the road.

The tanks for the reception of the rain-water running off the roads need not be deep, the space they would occupy would not be wasted, as they could be planted with the "Singhāra" (*Trapa bispinosa*), a species of water-nut which is much used by the natives as an article of food, and is eaten either raw, roasted (when it is not unlike the chestnut), or it is dried and ground into flour, when it is used mixed with water as a porridge, or made into cakes, in which form it is much eaten by Hindoos on fast days, when they are not by their religion allowed to eat their ordinary food. The edges of these tanks could be planted with the plantain or banāna, which is said by Humboldt and other authorities to produce a greater amount of food for man off a given area of land than any other plant. It is said "that an area of land which sown with wheat would feed only one man, would nourish five-and-twenty if planted with banānas." The above has reference to the fruit. The Bengalees also eat the inner part of the stem of the plant as a vegetable.

The plantain propagates itself by suckers, and its leaves and stem die away after it has borne fruit. In Upper India, where it is not much cultivated, after bearing fruit, the stem is cut down and allowed to rot on the ground, the natives not knowing how to utilize it; but the whole plant, stem and leaves, when chopped up, is readily eaten by cattle, and I hear the milch-cows in Calcutta are regularly fed on it. Whether this is the case or not I do not know, but I have for years given what I had in my garden to cattle as food without any injurious effects. The plantain being so useful both to man and beast, its propagation should be encouraged on all lands where it will grow. It flourishes best on low, moist lands, such as the borders of tanks, jheels and swamps, and a fringe of these plants round such places would prevent the spreading of malaria and render the neighbourhood more healthy. Care should be taken, in the first instance, to select plants bearing a good description of fruit, as there are some inferior sorts of plantain undistinguishable by the appearance of the plant which are perfectly useless as food, from the amount of seeds they contain. In a warm, damp climate the plantain will bear fruit in from one to one and a half years; in the dry climate of Upper India it does not bear under two or three years.

Another cause of surface-drainage originates in the higher lands. These lands may be twenty, fifty, or even a hundred feet higher than the level of the nearest rivers into which they drain. In former times these lands appear to have been regularly cultivated, and the fields composing them were separated from one another by ridges or banks, perhaps from one to two feet wide and six inches or a foot high, the remains of which can be distinctly traced where not too deeply covered with sand.

The higher parts of these lands—the water-shed—often consists of blowing sands, regular inland dunes, which are year by year increasing, and gradually covering the neighbouring fields. These dunes, composed as they are of loose, blowing sand, readily admit rain-water into them, and, except in heavy downpours, not much runs off the surface, where tolerably level; where, however, the surface of the land between the sandhills has become exposed by the blowing away of the drift-sand, it collects the water falling near, forms water-courses, and eventually ravines; the hardened surface, where exposed, is more like a concrete than a soil, and has the appearance and almost the density of sandstone. On digging into the sandhills we always find moisture present at a little depth below the surface: this water is not retained by resting on a stratum of clay or other impervious soil. If retained by an impervious stratum, we must suppose it to form a saucer-shaped depression, or escape of water would take place from its lower side. But these sandhills are elevated above the surrounding country, and there is no other way of accounting for their retaining water than by capillarity. Jheels, or swamps at the base of a range of sandhills, are fed by springs with water throughout the year, and never dry up, showing that all excess of water, beyond what can be held by capillarity, escapes by percolation.

Dunes occur in Europe, chiefly on the seashore; and centuries ago care was taken to encourage the growth of grass, chiefly the *Arundo arenaria*, on them. This grass binds the sand, and prevents its further drifting, and covering the neighbouring country.

Of such importance was this considered, that according to Marsh, in 1539, a decree of Christian III., King of Denmark, imposed a fine upon persons convicted of destroying certain species of sand-plants upon the coast of Jutland. This ordinance was renewed in 1558; and in 1569 the inhabitants were required to do their best to check the sand-drifts. In 1779 planting the *Arundo arenaria* and other sand-plants, and the exclusion of animals destructive to them, was adopted as a system. " Ten years later plantations of forest trees, which have since proved so valuable a means of fixing the dunes, and rendering them productive, were commenced, and have been continued ever since."

The planting of seashore dunes has been carried out in all European countries where they exist; the tree found most useful and best adapted for them being the *Pinus maritima*.

This tree has also in France been planted on inland dunes, and with equal success. The *Ailanthus glandulosa*, or Japan varnish-tree, has been successfully planted near Odessa for fixing dunes, and the tamarisk has also been recommended for that purpose.

Any tree that can be grown on these loose sands, as also grasses, will be useful and tend to bind them, and prevent their blowing over and covering the surrounding country; the chief thing after planting being to prevent destruction of the trees and grasses by cattle.

Where the land has not been reduced to the state of these dunes, we find it very much impoverished and perhaps uncultivated, or only cultivated at intervals of a few years with the inferior descriptions of grain in the rains. The surface-soil is sandy, but below a few inches of this sandy soil there is a firm substratum of stiffer earth. It appears as if the finer particles of the soil on the higher lands had been carried away by surface-drainage, and only the coarser gritty sand left behind. When this process has been going on for a long period, we have the dunes or sandhills, perfectly barren as far as regards producing food for man or cattle, and next the impoverished lands which only occasionally produce a crop of an inferior description of grain. On these lands the dunes are gradually encroaching; they are being reduced to the state of the dunes; and merely require time to become as useless agriculturally, unless steps are taken to prevent the spreading of the dunes.

In former times, when these lands were regularly cultivated, and the banks round the fields kept in repair, all rain falling on them must have been arrested by the loosened cultivated soil, and the ridges round the fields, either till it had time to sink into the soil too deeply to be evaporated, or would have been evaporated from the surface. There could have been no loss from surface-drainage as long as the ridges round the fields were in order and did their duty.

Now that these lands have been neglected, and the ridges have been allowed to fall out of order and become useless, the whole of the rain falling on them, with the exception of what is arrested by the looser sand, runs off by surface-drainage; the rush of water to the lower land is increased in both volume and force, and the land is cut into water-channels, by which, with the rush of water, the loosened surface-soil is carried away. The degradation of the surface-soil is shown by the trees on the high land, whose roots have been laid bare, and are now exposed above ground by the washing away of the surface-soil. With this, all manure and vegetable matters, such as the remains of stubble of former crops, leaves, &c., and lying on the surface, are carried away; the soluble salts of the dung and urine of cattle in the upper layers of the soil are also dissolved and washed out, and thus the soil of the country is robbed of its natural nourishment.

In every district a certain sum is set apart, under the name of the Road and Ferry Fund, for keeping in order the roads, and facilitating the means of internal communication. The roads, as I have said, are being more rapidly destroyed by surface-drainage than was formerly the case, and a yearly increasing sum has to be laid out in their repair and on bridges. The old bridges, which were formerly sufficient, are, now that surface-drainage has increased, found insufficient to carry off the water, and more extensive and expensive bridges have to be built in their places, and new bridges have to be built to cross watercourses which formerly did not exist. The roads are getting more difficult for conveyance of goods by wheeled carriages, and carriage by pack-animals may have ere long to be reverted to, if surface-drainage is allowed to go on increasing at the rate it has done of late years.

Besides the damage done to the higher lands by washing away their soil, carrying away the manure, &c., we must consider what are the results of this to the low-lying lands immediately below them, and in the smaller valleys of the watercourses, which carry their waters to the rivers, as also to the rivers themselves, and the countries through which they flow.

Where there are depressions on the surface of the country the rain-water finds its way to them, carrying with it the manurial matters that were on the surface of the drainage area. These depressions are known in India as jheels. The area of these jheels is considerably greater in the rains than at any other time of the year, from their spreading over the surrounding low-lying land. They are mostly shallow, are filled during and shortly after the rains with a dense growth of flags, bulrushes, and other aquatic plants in their shallower parts, and water-lilies where deeper. These plants die in the cold weather, the jheels gradually decrease, the water being lost by evaporation, or drawn off to irrigate the neighbouring fields, and the shallower jheels are altogether dried up during the hot weather. The decayed remains of the plants which grew in them, and the vegetable matters brought to them by surface-drainage, form a greasy, slimy mud, which, when exposed to the sun, on drying, causes malaria, and makes the surrounding country unhealthy.

The area of the land draining into the jheel may be five or ten times the area of the jheel itself. The drainage area cannot increase but by the action of water on the surface, the drainage channels to the jheel are improved, and the water falling on the drainage area more quickly finds its way to the jheel. With the water, besides the vegetable matter before mentioned, mineral soil is also carried down to the jheel, and it gradually silts up. Another cause of their filling up is found in the dust-storms of the hot weather.

It is probable that in former times these jheels were lakes of open water fringed with bulrushes and other aquatic plants, that they have been gradually getting shallower by silt, the dust deposited in them by dust-storms, and the decaying of the vegetation which was grown in them, and are now becoming the sources of disease, in proportion to the greater extent of their beds exposed to the influence of the sun's heat. As sheets of open water they might be innocuous, but it is the border of mud left by the drying up of the waters which appears to be the cause of malaria. The soil of the beds of these jheels is a sticky, slimy mud, containing a considerable amount of vegetable matter, and enriched with the exuviæ of numberless water-fowl.

The drainage of jheels has been proposed as a general measure, and in some instances has been carried out as a method of getting rid of the unhealthiness they cause. In Upper India, where it is said cultivation cannot be carried out without irrigation, on account of the dryness of the soil and climate, the soil and climate are to be made still more dry by *improved* surface-drainage. To drain these jheels an outlet must be made as deep as, or, where existing, must be lowered to the level of the lowest part of their beds.

The water coming into the jheel not being checked as before by being spread over a large area, will not deposit the various vegetable and mineral matters it contains in suspension, but will carry them through the drainage outlet with the rush of its stream; the outlet will be eroded and enlarged by the rush of water, which will further deepen the bed of the outlet, and the rich mud of the bed of the jheel will be carried away, to be deposited on the country lower down the stream, where on exposure it will cause malaria and disease. Disease in the neighbourhood of the jheel would temporarily be got rid of, —at the expense of increased disease to inhabitants of the country lower down the stream into which the jheel was drained, at the loss of valuable land which cannot be recovered, and water which is wanted on the higher lands would be more quickly conveyed away to the sea.

One newspaper, after describing the unhealthiness of parts of Oude from shallow jheels, advocated drainage of the jheels and low country, on the ground that drainage and quinine were supposed to be the only known remedies for fever and its attendant evils; and recommended irrigational canals (the Sardah Canal project in this case), for that very part of the country, on the ground that until it were irrigated by canals there would be no chance of drainage being carried out; showing drainage is considered a necessary sequel to irrigation by irrigationists. It does not seem to have occurred to the editor that prevention is better than cure, and that there might be a way of preventing the formation of jheels with their attendant fevers and ill effects, as effectual and valuable as vaccination is in preventing small-pox, and that this preventive remedy consists in accepting and taking advantage of rain, one of the most valuable gifts of the Almighty to man, and allowing it to sink into the earth where it fell, instead of spurning the precious gift and doing our utmost to get rid of it.

Floods in the Ganges and other Indian rivers are hailed in the newspapers, by a strange perversity of reasoning, as cheering assurances of rain having fallen further up country. Surely the sight of so much water running to waste, and damaging, instead of fertilizing the earth, should cause feelings of regret rather than of rejoicing.

Is Upper India suffering from an excess of moisture? If so, why extend irrigation? If not suffering from an excess of moisture, why resort to drainage? The fact is, that the water so much wanted is allowed to run to waste by streams, or is collected in hollows where it does harm, instead of being in the soil of the fields, where it is required for the crops; where Nature gave it and intended it should be used. It is in the wrong place.

A cubic foot of rain-water is said to contain, on an average, the following manurial matters:—

Nitrogen	10 to 12 grains.
Nitric acid, about ...	26 ,,
Ammonia ,, ...	5 ,,
Chlorine ,, ...	3 ,,
Magnesia ,, ...	3 ,,
Lime ,, ...	9 ,,

Every cubic foot of rain-water that runs off by surface-drainage is a loss of the above amount of manurial matters, which would, had the water sunk into the ground, have been retained in its upper layers available for the use of crops.

Nature knows best where water is wanted and ought to be, and deposits it over the whole country; cannot we carry out Nature's grand conception by assisting her to retain the water she gives where she places it?

Another result of draining the jheels would be that the fish in them, which supply a considerable amount of food to the neighbouring population, would be lost. The unhealthiness of these jheels, and the jheels themselves, are a result of surface-drainage; prevent the surface-drainage and the jheels will be reduced, and the unhealthiness caused by them will disappear.

I have mentioned on a previous page the ridges or small embankments round the fields, the remains of which are still traceable on the higher lands, showing they were formerly cultivated, and which are now used throughout the country as boundary-marks of the separate fields. These ridges, which are kept up more particularly on irrigated lands, are now simply the bounds defining the limits of the different fields, and are as narrow as they well can be, so as to occupy as small a space as possible.

It is possible that when these ridges were first brought into use it was with a view, not only of defining the limits of the fields, but of preventing the escape and flow of the rain-water; or, when only a small portion of the land of the country was cultivated, the latter may have been the only reason for making them.

Now with reference to jheels, if we want to prevent unhealthiness arising from them, we have merely to take measures to prevent their increased water area in the rainy season; and this can be done by banking up the fields of their drainage basins, in the way the natives ridge up their fields, taking care to do it effectually, so as to prevent surface-drainage. The operation should be commenced at the highest point or water-shed, and the different fields should be consecutively taken in hand to the edge of the jheel. In forming the banks, the soil to make them should be dug out from their lower sides, from pits; and not from ditches, which might become channels of surface-drainage: they should be made of sufficient width to withstand the water they may be required to hold back; of sufficient height to retain any probable heavy fall of rain; and on the upper side the soil should be filled in in a sloping direction to the top of the banks, so that the water should not lodge at their bases, but at some little distance from them. I have been told that if we retain the rain-water by banking up the fields we shall have the whole country under water, and that the whole country will suffer from fever, &c., as the low lands subjected to inundation now do.

The average annual rainfall throughout Upper India may be about 24 inches. Supposing it even to be 36 inches, and that the whole annual rainfall (which, however, is not the case) were precipitated in three months, from 20th June to 20th September, the rainfall would be 12 inches per month, less than three inches per week, and considerably less than half an inch per diem. If the soil were cultivated a foot deep, a large amount of the rain would be absorbed by the loosened soil, as it fell, as by a sponge, and some would be continually sinking into the subsoil by gravitation. As to the water penetrating the soil, causing fever, and rendering the higher lands as unhealthy as the lower lands now are, there does not seem to be much ground for this opinion, as where there are high lands with a loose soil, which arrests a larger proportion of the rain which falls on it, than the ordinary arable lands, and which escapes by percolation to the lower-lying lands or jheels instead of by surface-drainage, these high lands, known as *bhoor* lands, are remarkable as being the healthiest parts of the different districts in which they are. I am not aware of any case where water held in the soil by capillary attraction alone has been proved to be prejudicial to health.

The deeply-cultivated soil and the ridges would prevent loss of water from the surface of the land composing the drainage area of the jheel, would retain it where it fell, and the jheel would not be extended over the surrounding low-lying land in the rains. The deep cultivation, moreover, is a protection against loss of water by evaporation. When soil is deeply cultivated, rain falling on the surface passes through the loosened soil by gravitation, almost as soon as it falls on the surface; it gets under cover, and little is lost by evaporation.

It is universally admitted by agriculturists in all countries where farming has been studied as a science, and is not despised and left in the hands of the most ignorant of the population, as in India, that deep cultivation and pulverization of the soil preserve moisture in it. The reason of this, however, does not appear to be so well known as it deserves to be. It has been stated on a previous page that woods and forests preserve moisture, as their leaves falling on the ground retard surface-drainage, and hold water like a sponge. The trees act mechanically as a screen, they prevent the incidence of the sun's rays on the soil, and also break the force of the wind; thus the two great causes of evaporation are interfered with, and their effects moderated. In the case of lands deeply cultivated, and the soil thoroughly disintegrated and pulverized, the action is very similar. The greater part of the rain falling on the surface sinks quickly through the loosened soil, and is temporarily arrested by the soil underlying it, which gradually absorbs it under the pressure of gravitation, the remainder being held in the loosened, pulverized soil by capillarity. This water held by capillarity is evaporated by the action of the sun and winds, from the upper loosened soil, and as this becomes dry, it absorbs, by capillary attraction, more moisture from the moist stratum immediately below it. The height to which moisture will rise in loose, open, well-worked soils by capillary attraction is, however, very limited, and the loss from this cause would soon cease or be reduced to next to nothing. But as loss of moisture from this cause diminishes, another comes into operation,—the air penetrates the loosened soil, and when in the daytime it becomes heated, it expands, ascends, and carries off moisture in the form of vapour from the depths to which it had penetrated. During the night the reverse takes place; and as the loosened earth parts with the heat by radiation (which it had absorbed during the day) it is moistened by the vapour of water in the air which is condensed in and on it. The soil now, instead of being, as in the case of fields hardened with irrigation, an almost inert mass, has, as it were, become endowed with life, and acts as a breathing object, inhaling heat by day, exhaling it by night; abstracting from the air carbonic acid gas and ammonia, and both giving to and taking from it water.

The system of deep cultivation of the soil, and thus allowing the water to sink into it too deeply to be lost by evaporation, is that which, according to Marsh, was recommended by Palissy and Babinet for the formation of artificial springs. In the case of deep cultivation generally over a country, more especially a level country, there is a reservoir of water under every field, sufficient to supply the wants of vegetation held there by the soil itself. We enlist in our favour the powers of capillarity possessed by the soil. In what is the action of loosened soil different from that of forests in retaining moisture?

The upper loosened soil acts as trees do, and shades the soil below it. The loosened soil acts as a sponge, as the leaves of trees on the surface-soil of a forest do, and arrests the rain falling on it, and gives it time to sink under cover, and when the rain falling on the surface has sunk through the upper loosened soil it is as effectually protected from the evaporative influences of sun and wind as is water in the soil of a forest. The fact that leaves lying on the ground prevent evaporation of moisture from it, has led gardeners to employ leaves, straw, and other refuse vegetable matters to spread on the surface to keep the ground moist by preventing evaporation. This is called a mulch. Now, soil of every description, loosely spread on the surface, acts in the same way; but different soils do not act equally, and their powers of preventing loss of moisture by evaporation appear to be in inverse ratio to their powers of retaining heat. So humus, or decayed vegetable matter, which is placed at the bottom of Schubler's list of earths, would have the greatest power of preventing evaporation, and calcareous sand the least. The more humus, therefore, that there may be in a soil, the greater will be its power of preventing loss of moisture by evaporation. This, then, is another reason why, in *dry climates more particularly*, care should be taken to preserve and bury in the soil all refuse vegetable matters.

To return to our jheels. We have, by banking up the fields of their drainage basins, and by deep cultivation of them, the water in the subsoil instead of in or on the surface-soil merely. Once there and out of danger of loss by evaporation, the water will gradually find its way to the jheels by percolation or natural subsoil-drainage, which process will continue throughout the year; there will be a constant supply of water furnished to the jheel, which will be kept within more moderate limits in the rains, its bed will not be dried up and exposed to the action of the sun's heat in the dry seasons of the year, and thus we should get rid of a most fertile source of malaria, disease, and death. At the same time that excess of moisture would escape by percolation to the jheels, sufficient would be held in the soil for all the requirements of plants, by capillarity.

In the same way that water by surface-drainage finds its way to jheels, it also does to the minor water-courses, and eventually to the rivers; the drainage area is not increased, but the action of the water wears the surface-soil into slopes and channels, which facilitate the rush of the water; the beds of the water-courses and rivers are no longer able to carry off the water as quickly as it is brought to them, consequently they overflow their banks and spread over the low land near them. Over this land, out of the influence of the main current, the water is more sluggish, and it deposits on it the organic, vegetable and mineral substances it has brought down in suspension. As the floods subside, the action of the sun on the matters deposited by them causes malaria and disease, as in the case of jheels.

A marked case of this kind lately occurred in the district of Moradabad. The river Sote rises in that district, *in the plains*, and flows through the district of Budaon to the Ganges. In 1871 a part of the valley of this river in the Moradabad district became very unhealthy, nearly the whole of the population being prostrated with fever shortly after the end of the rains. On inquiry it appeared that the country on both sides of the river at that part was very low and flat; the valley below was rather contracted, the water could not run off as quickly as it was received, and the low flat land was under water for some time; this was where the unhealthiness was the greatest. Further down the river and all through the Budaon district, where the river keeps in a better defined channel, with more abruptly sloping banks, there was no unhealthiness in the valley of this river. I believe the drainage of the unhealthy part of the valley was proposed as a sanitary measure. If carried out, this will be another addition to the many causes we now have tending to desiccate the country and increase the violence and devastating power of the floods. Another case, and one of much greater importance, as affecting a larger extent of country and a greater population, is exactly similar, and that is Lower Bengal.

The same causes mentioned as affecting the climate in the neighbourhood of jheels, and in the case of the Sote river, are here at work, but on a more gigantic scale. The Ganges cannot carry off the water brought to it as quickly as it receives it; all Lower Bengal is flooded, and the results are fever and disease spread throughout the country. Increased, or, as it is called, *improved* surface-drainage in the drainage basin of the Ganges means increased desiccation of the part of the country where it is carried out, and increased floods and disease in Bengal. Every place drained will add its mite at the rate of *one hundred tons* of water for *every inch* of rainfall conducted to the Ganges from *every acre* of land whose surface-drainage is thus *improved.*

The evils in the case of Bengal are not only more extended and affect a greater population, but are more virulent, and should the fevers which have been ravaging the country for the last few years continue, large districts will be depopulated. Cholera is hardly ever absent from some parts of Lower Bengal which are liable to inundation. It often also originates at fairs held on the banks of rivers on lands subject to floods, and seems in many cases to spread up or down the courses of rivers. It appears to be a disease induced by filth and a saturated surface-soil, and it might well be that this disease would diminish were the low lands not so liable to inundation.

The drainage of Bengal has been proposed as a remedy. The operation would be a difficult and expensive one, as the country is almost a dead level; but supposing it done, how it would prevent floods the causes of which are some hundreds of miles away, does not appear; and how rice, the ordinary staple food-grain of Lower Bengal, and which requires water to grow in, is to be grown when the country is drained, is a mystery to me. The drainage of Bengal, however, is not required for the purpose of getting rid of the rain falling on Bengal itself, which is not in excess of its requirements, but to convey away the water of the floods which originated in Upper India and have been caused by improved surface-drainage there. Upper India, or at least that part of it included in the drainage basin of the Ganges, is being desiccated to swamp Bengal.

One cause of the greatly increased amount of fevers and unhealthiness of Bengal, in addition to the more rapid surface-drainage of the basin of the Ganges generally, which alone would cause higher floods, is the improved surface-drainage of the sites of towns and villages, and the land around them, as a sanitary measure, in Upper India. Near all towns and villages in Upper India there exist pits and hollows from which earth has been dug for building and other purposes. These are being drained to get rid of the filth deposited in and near them. As these pits and hollows have for ages been used as latrines, and are still so used, and as all the filth of the towns and villages drains to, and is accumulated in them, it is evident that the drainage of these low lands must throw a greater amount of filth into the rivers into which they are drained; this eventually finds its way into the Ganges, and may fairly be considered one cause of the increased unhealthiness of Bengal. This increased unhealthiness has only been noticed for a few years, probably since the time that the improved surface-drainage of towns has been in vogue as a sanitary measure. Quinine and drainage are recommended for Bengal as remedies for the fevers prevalent there. What can quinine and drainage effect when the causes of the evil are not interfered with, but are, on the contrary, being increased every day?

In the report of the Sanitary Commissioner of the North-Western Provinces for 1870-71, it is said in para. 37, "Sometimes indeed a good landlord, or the cultivators in combination, will make a good well, which, much frequented, soon becomes noted for its surrounding filthy moisture; for no care is given to drainage, excepting, perhaps, that whenever a resident finds accumulating water unpleasant, he endeavours to direct it to the first conveniently-situated lower-lying place at hand, without thought of his neighbours' rights or feelings."

Fault is found, and very properly, with people for getting rid of a nuisance by shunting it on their neighbours, but throughout the report we find improved surface-drainage to low grounds and rivers recommended as a means of getting rid of "hurtful or excessive moisture." If the moisture is "hurtful or excessive" on the high lands, it will be much more so on the low lands.

What is surface-drainage but increasing the pollution of the rivers, and as they fall into the Ganges, making it a main sewer. In the floods, the sewage-matter of the drainage basin of the Ganges is deposited on Bengal, and this is sufficient to account for the present unhealthy state of the country —increased floods and an increased amount of filth brought down by the floods; both the floods and the filth being the results of the so-called *improved* surface-drainage. It appears as if the "rights and feelings" of Bengal are not much considered by his neighbours in Upper India.* In the same way that the accumulation of water in the bed of a jheel, and its extending over the neighbouring low land in the rains, can be prevented, and its bed kept from drying up in the hot weather, so also can floods in rivers during the rains be prevented, and greater depth of water kept up in them during the dry seasons of the year, and that way is by retaining the rain-water *in* the soil *on* which it fell, preventing its escape by surface-drainage, and permitting it only to find its way to lower land and streams, filtered by percolation (natural subsoil drainage) through the soil. The rivers would remain at a more equable depth throughout the year, which would greatly facilitate their navigation, and many of the smaller streams, only occasionally used for navigation during the rains, would be navigable throughout the year.

The Ganges and Jumna rise in the Himalayas, and after a comparatively short course in the hills, enter the plains, flow separately to Allahabad, where they join, and then run to the sea.

The volume of water of these rivers and their tributaries where they issue from the hills, is a mere fraction of the

* *See* Appendix B, p. 101.

amount conveyed by the Ganges through its various mouths to the sea. The greater part of this vast volume of water has fallen on the plains of the drainage basin of the Ganges, and if the system I have described of banking up the fields were carried out throughout the country, so as to prevent surface-drainage, we should hear no more of floods and the damage done by them.

It is only two or three years since the towns of Jounpore and Azimgurh, on two separate rivers, both rising in the plains, were nearly washed away by floods which must have originated in the plains, a clear proof that improved surface-drainage is not required in that part of the country. Besides the more notorious cases of damage by floods, such as the carrying away of towns and villages, the cutting away of lands, railway embankments, and bridges, and the fevers and other illnesses caused by their drying up, there are other evils the results of floods which are not so generally known. Large areas of land which only a few years ago used amongst other produce, to carry rain crops, are now never sown with those crops, as the land has now, by increased surface-drainage higher up the country become so liable to inundation, that the risk of loss from that cause is greater than the prospect of gain. The cultivation is not safe. It is too much of a gambling transaction, with heavy odds against the cultivator who is rash enough to try it.

The districts of Seharunpore and Mozuffurnuggur, where irrigation from the Ganges Canal has been largely practised of late years (the canal was opened about twenty years ago), have become notoriously unhealthy, and special inquiries and reports have been made on the causes of the unhealthiness of these districts, which previous to the opening of the canal were as healthy as any in Upper India, in fact, were favourite districts. The results of the inquiries and reports is a recommendation that these districts, which formerly did not suffer from excess of water, should have their suface-drainage, or natural drainage channels improved. This is being done, and the result must be that the rain falling on these districts, or such part of them as have their surface-drainage *improved*, will more quickly find its way to the rivers, and will cause greater floods lower down country and greater damage to Bengal. " Improved surface-drainage," however, is the popular cry of the present time in India. The result of increased drainage facilities near the sources of streams, must be that their beds, which are adapted to carry away a given amount of water gradually finding its way to them, cannot hold the same amount suddenly brought to them, the water must spread and overflow the low-lying lands near them, the banks of the rivers must get worn away by erosion, the rivers get choked up with the silt they have brought down, the *débris* of the land they have ruined; this raises their beds and reduces the amount of water they are able to carry to the sea, whilst an increased amount is brought to them, causing the floods to extend over an increased area; bars form across their mouths, and their navigation becomes more and more difficult and dangerous.

The heat and consequent aridity of the climate (so far as they are due to surface-drainage), will decrease, as surface-drainage is lessened, as will also its other ill consequences, *e.g.* floods and their attendant evils, &c. On the contrary, as surface-drainage is increased, or as it is now the fashion in India to say, improved, all these evils will be exaggerated. Every single field from which loss of water by surface-drainage is prevented, will tend to lessen the ravages of floods.

Every inch of rainfall lost by surface-drainage from every acre of ground, represents a loss of one hundred tons of water to that acre; water which that acre (in Upper India at least, and in all countries where during the year there are long periods of dry weather) can ill afford to lose. The average loss of water by surface-drainage throughout the country is probably half the rainfall, but supposing it to be ten inches, then the loss per acre would be one thousand tons or 640,000 tons per square mile, which increases the floods.

There are many thousands of square miles of country within the drainage basin of the Ganges that could be made safe against famine and the effects of droughts by taking care of the rainfall; and at the same time the climate of Upper India would be improved, and floods and their ill effects would be no more known throughout the lower lands and in Bengal. One of the ill effects of floods in Bengal is, that the banks which are made round the rice-fields to retain the rainfall, are broken by the rush of the flood-water, and are thus rendered unable to retain sufficient either of the flood-water, or the rain which falls on the land, for the wants of the rice crop.*

From the foregoing pages it will be seen that it is during the hot weather, when the capacity of the atmosphere for holding the vapour of water in suspension is at its maximum, and when the air would be most cooled by evaporation from the surface of the earth, solar heat being expended in evaporation, that the minimum amount of moist evaporative surface is presented to the influence of the rays of the sun. There is next to no vapour in the atmosphere to moderate the force of the direct rays of solar heat falling on the surface of the earth, which being exposed to their unmitigated heat becomes excessively heated, and heats the air coming in contact with it. Any method by which we can increase the evaporative surface of the country, and diminish the extent of its bare reflective surface, will tend to diminish the heat of its climate. Trees and vegetation of any kind will do this, in so far as they shade the ground from the direct rays of the sun, and

* *See* Appendix C, p. 102.

prevent its becoming heated; they also absorb heat during the day, which they give off by radiation at night, and they transpire from their leaves the moisture which they imbibe by their roots from the lower-lying moist strata of the earth, which in the form of vapour in the atmosphere moderates the amount of solar heat falling on the ground.

Supposing the country to be divided like a chess-board, the squares of say a mile each in measurement, the black squares planted with trees and bushes, and the white squares left bare for cultivation, arable land, the planted squares would absorb a great amount of the solar heat which fell on them, and the air in the daytime above them would not be so hot as that coming in contact with the surface of the bare squares. The cooler air over the planted squares would by its greater gravity sink and displace the air over the bare squares as it became heated and expanded. At night, the heat absorbed by the planted squares during the day would be given off by radiation, the superincumbent air would be chilled, sink, and spread over the surface of the bare squares, displacing the more heated air which had not been chilled by radiation. The trees on the planted squares would act mechanically in checking and breaking the force of the wind, as a lattice-work breakwater breaks the force of the waves; they would also deflect the wind upwards; it would not sweep over the surface of the bare squares as it does over a plain where there is nothing to check its force, and its drying effects would be lessened. The surface-soil of the bare squares would not be so dried and hardened from the action of the wind as the open plain now is; the air would contain more vapour of water evaporated from the trees of the planted squares; and this again would interpose a screen which would lessen the amount of solar heat falling on the surface of the bare squares. The soil of the bare squares not being so dried and hardened could be ploughed and broken up at any season of the year, which now it cannot be, owing to its hardened condition; and when broken up, it too would further help to moderate the heat of the hot weather by its increased absorptive and radiative powers.

It is universally admitted by all physicists that the presence of forests and trees tends to equalize the temperature of a country throughout the year; that the summers are not so hot, and the winters not so cold, as in a country devoid of trees. I have shown how it would affect the summer heat. The chief reasons of the winters not being so cold is the retarded radiation of heat from the ground under the trees, caused by their foliage and branches. When, however, in consequence of the presence of trees, the bare fields were broken up and made absorptive and radiative, it might be considered that the heat caused by arrested radiation from the ground under the trees might be counteracted by the increased radiation from the bare land. This is a problem that has not, as far as I am aware, been solved as yet, and must depend greatly on the relative proportions of the wooded and bare lands. As radiation of heat from the bare lands would be moderated by the amount of vapour in the atmosphere, and the vapour in the atmosphere in dry climates is mainly derived by evaporation from the leaves of trees, it is evident that the greater the proportion of wooded land the less would be the loss of heat by radiation at night from the bare land.

The greater the proportion of land covered with trees the more will the country be cooled during summer by its effects. If the uncultivated lands now lying useless, and which are obnoxious to the climate, were planted, one of the chief immediately remediable sources of heat would be obliterated, and we should in its stead have a source of coolness from the amount of heat used up in the evaporation of moisture from the leaves of the trees; and the amount of vapour in the air from the evaporation would lessen the amount of solar heat falling on the surface of the earth. The extent of the surface of the earth exposed to the direct action of solar heat would be lessened, and the exposed surface would be less heated. If it is admitted that the hot west winds are the results of the heating of the surface of the earth by the direct incidence of the rays of the sun, it must follow that they would be moderated in proportion to the reduced surface area exposed to the action of the sun, and to the lessened heating of that surface. Should there still be west winds, the trees would mechanically break their force and deflect them upwards; their sweeping, drying effects on the surface would be less; the ground would not be so hardened in the hot weather as it now is, and the vapour in the air, now carried away to the east by the strong west winds, would, as the winds became more moderated or subdued, remain suspended over the country, and be present in the superincumbent air to be deposited as dew or rain.

The statement is frequently made that the hot west winds are useful in keeping houses and buildings cool by promoting evaporation from tatties, &c. What is this but an admission that the hot winds are useful to this extent—that we can in houses, by their means, moderate the heat that has created them, and which they themselves intensify. Also that some method of cooling houses is, under existing circumstances, necessary, and in the case of tatties this is done by evaporation, which moistens the air in the houses.

In the case of a well-wooded country the result is the same —the evaporation cools the air. It is common in describing a place to say it is green and cool-looking. This combination of greenness and coolness is not altogether imaginary, as some people think. The fresh verdure of vegetation is a great absorbent of heat; and moisture, which cools the surrounding air, is largely evaporated from fresh young leaves. These effects are lessened as the leaves lose the freshness of youth, fade, and dry up. Young leaves have a soft, yielding surface, and are filled with sap; as they become older they become harsh and crisp to the touch, and lose their power of absorbing and radiating heat; they also contain less sap, and can give up but a reduced amount by evaporation; hence the effect of forests and vegetation in cooling the air is greater immediately after the trees are fresh clothed with new leaves in spring than when the leaves are drying up and dying.

Besides the influence of trees in moderating the extremes of heat and cold of the climate of a country, there is the influence they exert on the rainfall. I have stated that the rainfall in the Dooab is small in comparison with that of the Teraee and southern slopes of the Himalayas. Forests and vegetation, by radiation, cool the air, and the cooled air coming into contact with warm air laden with humidity, causes condensation, and the vapour of water in the air is precipitated. The greater rainfall of the Teraee and southern slopes of the Himalayas is due to the greater amount of radiation caused by the forests there. The clouds laden with vapour pass over the bare plains without discharging their moisture, because there is a want of absorptive and radiative power, and the air above them not being cooled by radiation, the clouds do not part with their moisture, but retain it till they reach a place where such chilling of the air by radiation occurs, which they find over the Teraee and the southern slopes of the Himalayas. The rank vegetation of the Teraee, and its unhealthiness, are due to the greater precipitation of rain and accumulation of water in the vegetable soil from surface-drainage. By planting the uncultivated lands of the plains with trees, and thus making the surface of the country more absorptive and radiative, the clouds in passing over it, coming in contact with the chilled air, would part with more of the water with which they are charged, and less would remain to be precipitated over the Teraee and southern slopes of the Himalayas, and the rainfall would be more equally distributed over the whole country. The moisture, instead of being retained in the clouds until it fell in torrents, would be more frequently precipitated, the showers would be more frequent, and milder in their character. There would be frequent gentle, soaking showers, instead of occasional torrents of rain.

The action of deeply-cultivated soil in chilling the air and causing precipitation must be the same as that of forests. A solid, firm soil, saturated with water, is a bad absorbent and radiator of heat. Break up the soil deeply, so that rain falling on it may sink quickly to the subsoil, and that the surface-soil may not remain so saturated, and may be more quickly dried by evaporation, and we shall then find that, by its increased powers of absorption and radiation of heat, it will act in the same way as forests in cooling the temperature of the country in the rains and in promoting rainfall.

The extent of barren lands—lands formerly cultivated, but now producing no crop, save, perhaps, some poor grass in the rains, is increasing every year.

The causes of the increase of these barren lands are numerous. On the high land we have the sandhills or dunes, which are yearly extending and spreading over the neighbouring fields; the oosur plains consisting of a hard soil, with a saline efflorescence which sterilizes them; the ravines, the results of surface-drainage, by which the land is carried away; and the lands covered with reh by irrigation. Besides the improvement to the climate which would accrue from planting these now useless lands, there are other benefits of no small importance which nature has pointed out.

Where land is allowed to remain undisturbed by man, and cattle are not allowed to graze on it, in course of time it becomes covered with grasses, trees, and shrubs. The grasses as they die, and the leaves falling on the land, enrich the soil, and render it more fertile than it formerly was. When forest land is broken up the surface-soil is found richer, and produces better crops without manure than land which has been some lengthened time under cultivation. This is due to the accumulation of vegetable matter in the upper layers of the soil; the leaves, &c., which have rotted on it and become converted into humus or vegetable mould, and the roots which have penetrated the deeper layers of the soil and have forced apart its particles have made it more loose and porous, and the smaller root-fibres or rootlets have also on rotting become humus.

Having this evidence before us of the results of forest growth, we can easily imagine what would be the ultimate effects on the soil of planting barren lands with trees. The first expense may, while these lands are in the hands of impoverished landlords, be the chief obstacle; the expense, however, would be a mere trifle, as most of the trees grow well from seed sown on the spot, and no transplanting is needed. But as trees grow very rapidly in Upper India, and wood for all purposes sells at a very high rate, particularly where the barren lands are chiefly situated, and where there is no wood grown on the spot, the expenses would soon be recovered, the return would be sharp.

Wood is largely used as fuel by the railways for locomotives, and has to be brought from a distance, which is steadily increasing, and costing more for carriage. The natives can only at high prices obtain the wood required in constructing their houses. Even a thatched shed requires a ridge-pole, and bamboos or some substitute for them for the framework of the thatch. The trees best suited for planting, and which besides improving the land would be of value as timber, are the babool, sissoo or sheesham, the saras mango, mulberry, neem, and bēr. One of the most common substitutes for bamboos in the frames of thatches is the stalk of the castor-oil plant, and this plant requires some consideration. It will grow almost anywhere, and is in many ways of great economic value. Besides the stalks being used as above stated, they are also used in flat-roofed houses as battens, the oil is largely used as a lubricant by the railways, and now that gas is made from oil-cake, the refuse cake, which is useless or poisonous as a cattle-food, could be used for gas manufacture, as also could the nut itself before the oil was extracted from it. The leaves are to some extent gathered and given to cattle as food, although said not to be good for them in large quantities, still, wherever any castor-oil plants are accessible to cattle, we find all the leaves are eaten off in the hot weather. One advantage of this plant is its rapid growth, plants attaining a height of ten or fifteen feet by the month of April from seed sown the previous June or July. This plant will live some ten or more years, and propagates itself by the seeds which fall from it; once sown it only requires to be protected from the depredations of cattle. Advantage should be taken of the rapid growth of this plant to use it as a nurse to trees of more delicate habit. The mango, for instance, for the first few years after being planted out, is usually protected by being tied up in long grass during the cold weather to protect it from frost. Were the castor-oil plant thickly studded over the ground between the young mango plants they would be as effectually protected from frost as they now are, and in the spring their leaves would not have the pale sickly hue the trees have which have been protected by being wrapped up in grass.

As the castor-oil plant bears fruit within six months after being sown, and continues to bear annually, extensive cultivation of it might be remunerative. I have, however, never seen a good-sized field of it in Upper India. There is often a row sown by the side of sugar-cane fields, where it is treated as an annual, and cut down in March or April; and it is grown about gardens and in villages occasionally, and it is in villages on high sandy land, where the finest specimens of the plant are to be seen, which show to what size it will grow if protected from cattle, and with what ease the sandhills and barren land might be covered with it.

There would be but little difficulty in inducing growth of trees, &c., on the high sandy lands. As I have said before, water is present in them throughout the year, and is not lost by capillary attraction and evaporation; and the prevention of surface-drainage would enable trees to grow more rapidly on them. Small pits dug for the seed to be deposited in, or for young plants, is all the digging necessary. On the harder soils the whole ground should be deeply dug or trenched, to prevent loss of water by capillary attraction, in addition to making banks to prevent surface-drainage. In England it is recommended to dig deeply, or trench the whole of a piece of ground on which it is intended to plant timber or forest trees, in preference to merely making pits for the several trees. It is said that by digging or trenching the whole ground the trees are not so liable to suffer should dry seasons occur after they have been planted out. If in the rains we cultivate a field deeply, and break up and pulverize the soil finely so as to leave no clods, we shall find more moisture in the soil within a few inches of the surface, throughout the succeeding hot weather, than in the soil of a field not so broken up.

The law of capillarity of soils, not yet sufficiently studied or understood as far as I am aware, by which a fixed percentage of moisture is retained in the soil where deeply cultivated, within a varying depth from the surface, which depth is governed by the nature of the soil and the state of the atmosphere, requires some consideration. The lower parts of a deeply-loosened soil being pressed together by the weight of the superincumbent soil, are more able to raise water by capillary attraction from the wet subsoil, and to retain it, than the upper parts which are not so pressed together, and are less liable to loss of moisture from evaporation than the upper layers of the soil which cover and protect it. The greater the power of retaining water possessed by the soil the nearer the surface will any fixed percentage of water be found; and it will be found nearer the surface during a humid than in a dry state of the atmosphere.

Cases are common in England where the surface of the ground, which keeps perfectly dry during a continuance of dry weather, becomes wet on the approach of rain, and water oozes out. During the dry weather the ground is kept dry by evaporation of the water, as it rises to the surface by capillary attraction. On the approach of rain, the air being more humid, there is less evaporation, and the surface is wet. People who have not before seen it are astonished on being shown the amount of moisture present in May and the earlier part of June previous to the rains, in Upper India, within a few inches from the surface, in soils which were deeply dug in the preceding rains, which have been well pulverized, and have not become caked into masses. The loosened layer of surface-soil acts as a mulch, the particles of soil being more widely separated, the water cannot rise by capillary attraction to the surface, as it does where the particles are closer together.

At one time I thought moisture might rise through a pulverized soil sooner than through a denser, and that advantage might be taken of it to carry out a system of subsoil irrigation, by which water might be economized, and at the same time the surface-soil not be hardened. On a lawn which had been regularly irrigated, and the soil hardened, I dug drains, laid down tiles, and filled in the drains with the loose soil. The tiles were laid some fifteen inches below the surface, and were loosely put together, so that water might easily escape. I made a reservoir, and the drains all branched from it; and from the reservoir all the drains could be supplied with water. It was reversing the system of subsoil drainage. The drains were to convey water to the subsoil and irrigate it, instead of conveying water from the subsoil and making it dry. In practice I found the surface of the soil over the drains was dry, but the surface on both sides at a little distance from the drains was wet; the moisture rose to the surface where the soil was hard and consolidated, and was then exposed to evaporative influences, but it had not risen to the surface where the soil was loose—this showed the difference in the power of capillary attraction possessed by the same soil under the different conditions of pulverization and consolidation.

On a previous page, after stating how trees had been killed by heat in the Budaon district in 1868 and 1869, I said it was remarkable the trees so killed were on low land with a hardened surface-soil, and no trees were killed on the high lands with a loose sandy surface-soil.

The spring level being nearer the surface-soil of the low lands than of the high lands, it might be supposed the trees would suffer on the low lands to a less extent than on the higher land; but we find the reverse to be the case. The increased amount of moisture rising to the surface in hardened soils by capillarity and being carried away by evaporation, accounts for the greater damage done to trees and vegetation generally during a season of drought on lands with a hard consolidated soil, and in the case I have adduced killed large trees.

In lands of this description the leaves, if not taken away for fuel or other purposes, are liable, owing to the smooth, hardened state of the soil, to be blown away. Digging the soil occasionally—the deeper the better—and burying in it all leaves, twigs, &c., lying on the surface, so as to keep it open, would, by preventing loss of moisture by capillary attraction, ensure the safety of trees from death by drought.

In planting trees in hard land, more particularly in hot dry climates, it is advisable to dig deeply or trench the whole ground; for this reason, that the water sinking into the soil is not so soon lost as when only pits are dug for the trees. If the trees are planted at two yards apart, and pits are dug a yard square, only one-fourth of the land is dug. Through the undug hard soil the moisture will rise by capillary attraction, and will also abstract the water from the dug portion of the land, and none will remain for the trees, which will suffer in consequence.

Irrigation primarily from wells and afterwards from canals was designed with the best intentions and hopes of success—to prevent famines, to counteract the effects of droughts, to insure good crops, and cheap food for the population, to bring into cultivation land supposed to be unculturable from want of water; and it was further supposed that a good return in cash as interest would be made for the money spent on irrigational works.

What has irrigation done for the country? It has signally failed to do all that was foretold of it. Famines have been more frequent and more severe since canals were made. Droughts are greater than they previously were. The air of the whole country is more arid and injurious to animal and vegetable life than it formerly was, from the cutting down of forest trees, &c., for burning bricks and lime for the canals and other canal purposes, and to clear land for irrigation. A great amount of land has become covered with *reh*, and is by many persons considered to be permanently sterilized. There is very good reason to fear there is not a single acre of land that has been irrigated by canals for ten years, whose produce has not very considerably diminished.

The prices of food-grains and all agricultural produce are notoriously higher than they were. The price of labour is consequently raised, the cost of all public and private works very much increased, and the poorer classes generally are worse off. Add to these the fevers and consequent prostration of the inhabitants of the districts longest irrigated by canals, where we are told the population is decreasing, the men having become emasculated, &c., from the effects of fevers and other diseases caused by irrigation.* In the face of these facts, there are people who still talk of the so-called *blessings* of irrigation. Are these blessings, or are they curses?

Irrigation, by canals, although for the first two or three years after it has been brought into play, it increases the crops, eventually reduces the productive powers of the land; and I have frequently heard it stated by natives that where irrigation from canals has superseded dry cultivation, and has been carried on for ten years, the produce is reduced to less than it was before irrigation was resorted to; and there is not a single field the yearly produce of which is as much after ten years canal irrigation as it was before on the dry system. That the produce of canal-irrigated lands does fall off, after the first few years of irrigation, is not denied:† it is admitted by the advocates of irrigation, who say this is the result of

* Dr. Cutliffe's report on certain districts of the Meerut divison.
† *See* Appendix D, p. 102.

overcropping the land; crops being taken from the land in more rapid succession than was formerly the case; and the fact of its never being allowed to lie fallow has exhausted the land. If, however, this were the real reason, land must very soon become exhausted by bearing crops; but experiments have been carried on in England where land has been cropped with wheat for twenty years in succession, without manure, and on which there has not been any material diminution of the crop.

These experiments were made with the express purpose of finding out to what extent the soil was deprived of its elements of fertility by continuous growth of crops without being manured, and the result has shown that under cropping lands do not so rapidly become exhausted as was formerly believed to be the case.

The real reason of the falling off in the produce of canal-irrigated lands appears to be the consolidation of the pan by the treading of the cattle in ploughing and the hardening of the upper soil by irrigation. This causes shallower ploughing, the roots of plants have less depth of soil in which to search for food, and cannot force their way into the hardened pan; and there is the alternate soaking and drying of the land, during which the natural salts of the earth are gradually brought nearer the surface by capillary attraction.

This process may go on for some years before the land shows any excessive amount of reh on the surface; but the soil is steadily being poisoned by its accumulation in the upper soil, which accounts, together with the increased hardness of the soil, for the diminished fertility of lands some time under irrigation.

Irrigation merely acts as a stimulant for a short time, and eventually reduces the productive powers of the land. This could be tested by comparing the produce of lands for the first few years after irrigation with the produce of similar lands which have been irrigated by canals ten or twenty years, and also comparing the produce with the amount of seed sown in these lands and in unirrigated lands. If it is found that the produce and proportion of it to seed sown is less on land that has been irrigated for some length of time than on land recently brought under irrigation, it may safely be inferred that irrigation is doing more harm than good to the country.

I have shown how irrigation, by hardening the surface-soil, acts injuriously on the climate by increasing the heat; it also, by hardening and condensing the soil, and preventing the rain falling on the surface sinking into the ground, increases surface-drainage, and assists the desiccation of the country by the water in the soil being better able to rise in the condensed soil by capillary attraction than in a soil not so consolidated. The harder and more compact the soil becomes, the less moisture is found in the subsoil, say one or two feet below the surface, after a lengthened period of dry weather.

The increase of indigo cultivation in the Upper Dooab, and its successful prosecution there, is advanced as an argument in favour of canal irrigation. Here is an extract of a letter from an indigo-planter in that part of the country to another indigo-planter on the subject:—

"The produce in canal-irrigated lands, in my opinion, will be worse yearly; what with sowing the same seed, and with this constant cropping and flooding, the lands are being thoroughly exhausted. I remark yearly a great falling off of leaf, and this, by the bye, appears to be increasing. Canal plant grows too quickly; it is, in fact, forced, and it consequently cannot draw sufficient support from the soil fast enough to keep pace with its rapid growth. If I am right in my conjecture, produce will get worse as the soil becomes more exhausted," &c.

The opinion here given of a man who has been engaged for many years in the indigo line does not agree with that of people who talk of the successful growth of indigo in the Upper Dooab.

One of the arguments brought forward in favour of irrigation is, that there is an increasing demand for water where canals have been established: this is brought forward by irrigationists as evidence that the native cultivators are beginning to appreciate irrigation. This increased demand for water is caused by the increased impermeability of the soil to water, and by its being more quickly evaporated from the surface, where it is more speedily brought by capillary attraction. The greater amount of water supplied to the land the more it will require.

With greater power of capillarity the natural soluble salts of the soil are more quickly brought in solution to the surface, where they remain when the water is lost by evaporation; and some salts are brought to the land in the water used for irrigation.

We never see reh on the higher lands, which are generally of a lighter and more sandy description, and being so, are more porous; it is always on land subjected to irrigation, either artificial or natural, or with a hard soil that we find reh.* The naturally irrigated lands are those lower lands on which water is deposited by surface-drainage from the higher lands. It appears here, also, as if two causes were at work. The salts of the higher lands may be brought down in a state of solution or suspension, and deposited, and the natural salts of the lower lands may rise in the soil in solution by capillary attraction. There are many well-known cases of inland seas and lakes—the Dead Sea, the Caspian, and the Aral, the waters of which are more impregnated with saline matters

* The *oosur* lands are of the latter description.

than the ocean. These seas have no outlet, and the greater amount of salt in their waters is the result of evaporation of the water brought down to them, the salts brought down in the water from the drainage basin of the rivers pouring into them being left behind. The two former seas are below the sea-level. The same is the case of inland lakes, many of which are considerably above the sea-level, but which have no surface exit for the water brought to them, and which is lost by evaporation. The percentage of saline matters in these inland seas and lakes is greater than in the ocean.

There are many cases of land which being under water during the rainy seasons, dries up, and is covered with a saline incrustation during the dry weather. These are temporary shallow lakes, which lose their water in the hot seasons by evaporation, the salts being left behind when the water is evaporated.

Where these salt lakes and plains are below the level of the sea, their existence there is said to be due to a subsidence of the crust of the earth; and where above the sea-level, they are considered to be the beds of ancient seas, elevated by upheaval. Is this true in every case? May it not be that in many cases these salt lakes and plains below the sea level are the result of evaporation? Should the amount of water lost by evaporation from a lake exceed the amount supplied to it from its drainage area, the area of the lake would contract till an equilibrium was established between the amount of water received by drainage and that expended by evaporation. In the case of plains which dry up, there can be no excess of evaporation over amount of water supplied; the last drop of moisture is dried up, and there the matter ends till there is a fresh supply. Where salt plains occur above the sea-level they may be the result of the gradual elevation of the land by silt brought down from higher lands. The accumulation of saline matters on their surface is the residue of evaporation, the greater part being due to the rising, by capillary attraction, of the salts brought down to them from the higher lands in former times. The beds of all lakes must in the same way be gradually rising, from the amount of earthy matter brought to them with the water from higher lands. Should, by any convulsion of nature, the outlets of the Red Sea become closed, and it be converted into an inland lake, it is easy to suppose its level would be reduced to below the ocean-level, from the amount of evaporation from its surface exceeding the amount of water supplied to it by rivers and springs. This lowering of the surface would go on till in the course of time the surface area was contracted and an equilibrium established between the amount received from rivers and springs (*i. e.* surface and underground drainage) and the amount lost by evaporation.

In the case of land irrigated from canals the same causes are at work; the rain which falls on the hills and other elevated lands is diverted into the canals and distributed over the land, carrying with it what amount of salts it may contain. The percentage of salts in the water may be small, but if it is in excess of the amount required and taken up by the crops grown on the land, it will continue increasing until from its excess it becomes injurious.

The fact, however, remains that lands subjected to irrigation in Upper India, more especially to irrigation from canals, become after some time covered with reh. On analysis it is found that reh may be composed—

    1st. Entirely of carbonate of soda; or,
    2nd. Of carbonate and sulphate of soda; or,
    3rd. Of carbonate and sulphate of soda and chloride of
        sodium.

All these salts are more or less useful to vegetation; it is only when they are in excess that they are injurious. They have been used as manures; their effects have been more marked and beneficial on light sandy soils than on soils of a more clayey description; their having a greater effect on the light lands shows those lands were deficient in these salts, and as the light sandy soils are in general higher than the stiffer clayey soils, it favours the opinion I have given that these salts may have been washed out of the higher lands. If such is the case, transferring the reh from lands where it is in excess, and using it as a manure on the light sandy lands where it is deficient, would benefit both descriptions of land. Acting on this I last year tried reh as a manure on several fields of wheat and barley on high sandy land, in each case giving a top-dressing to half of each field. In each field the effect was very conspicuous, the parts manured with the reh were more luxuriant, and the line was well defined where the manured and unmanured parts of the field met.

In spite, however, of the general increase of reh on irrigated lands, which I am glad to see is now exciting attention, further irrigational projects have been sanctioned and are being carried out. The injury done to the country by irrigation cannot be denied, still, the suicidal system is to be persisted in, as will be seen by the following extract from a resolution of the Government of India, headed " Forecasts of Expenditure on Railways and Irrigation Works."

" IRRIGATION WORKS."

" The total expenditure required is estimated at £20,325,000. Of this sum £4,589,000 has already been spent, and during the next six years, including 1872-3, the outlay will be about £8,489,000; of this last amount £625,000 will be paid by the Puttiala and other Sikh States, and the balance of £7,864,000 must be raised by loan, or paid from surplus of ordinary revenue over expenditure."

It also appears that during the next five years 50,000 square miles of country are to be secured from liability to drought by irrigation works ! ! !

Will not these 50,000 square miles be covered with reh and be a desert twenty years hence? Why should the result of irrigation on these lands be different to what we have seen on similar lands? What is to be expected from increased irrigation, but, amongst other ill results, an increased area of land rendered sterile by reh? Man in each succeeding generation has but a life-interest in the land, and has merely a right to the produce of it; he has no right to spoil the land, to spend the principal, but is bound in honour to leave it in as good a state for posterity, as that in which he received it from his ancestors, to live, in fact, on the interest nature gives. Shall we in India leave the land in as good and fruitful a state for our successors as that we received it in from our predecessors? We see the land gradually being rendered unfit for cultivation, a steady deterioration taking place, and still we persevere in the system which is rendering it unculturable. When posterity finds the diminished culturable area of the country insufficient to supply its wants, it will pass rather a harsh judgment on the acts of the present generation by which its food supplies have been reduced.

There is now a famine impending, the population is crying for food, and we persist in irrigation, which, by its injurious action on the country, further diminishes the supply of food

I do not know when irrigation from wells, as a method of growing ordinary grain crops, was first established in Upper India, but it has latterly been considered that water was the one thing required.

In the earlier part of the present century there was not that care taken to provide water for agricultural purposes, nor was there that anxious solicitude about the rainfall there now is, and which may be said to have reached a state of chronic alarm.

There was a famine—a very severe one—in 1837 or 1838, which prevailed more especially in the Dooab, or country between the Ganges and the Jumna. This tract of land between these rivers was then, as now, more bare of trees than the country immediately north of the Ganges, and irrigation from wells was here in vogue before it was established in Rohilcund. I was told some two or three years ago by some zemindars of the Budaon district in Rohilcund that some fifty or sixty years previous there was no irrigation in their part of the district. "It might have been used," they said, "by gardeners for vegetables, but was never attempted, or even thought of, for grain crops. In those days there were no famines; but now, since irrigation has increased, famines are continually recurring; the cattle, too, in former days did not suffer for want of forage, whereas numbers now die annually from want of food."

This being stated by different men in different parts of the district, showed that irrigation must have been unknown throughout the district for corn crops at the time they alluded to, fifty or sixty years ago. The Settlement Records of the district show that at the former settlement of 1835, only 4,991 acres were irrigated to 633,590 unirrigated, or 1 to 126; while at the settlement lately concluded, 202,505 acres are irrigated to 629,528 unirrigated, or 1 to 3.

Irrigation from wells in the Budaon district is said to have been introduced by emigrants from the Dooab, where it had been earlier practised. It would be interesting to learn when irrigation from wells originated in the Dooab—probably it was pretty general previous to the famine of 1837 or 1838.

Irrigation from wells would, in a country where shallow cultivation of the soil is the rule, have the effect for some time of increasing the produce of the land. Seeing this, the cultivators would migrate from the higher lands, where the spring level of the water was at a greater depth from the surface, and where, from the looser and more sandy nature of the soil and subsoil, the wells were more liable to fall in,—to the lower lands, where the spring level of the water was nearer the surface, where the wells would not require to be so deep, and where, from the greater firmness of the soil, the wells were not so liable to fall in as on the higher lands. The diminished fertility of the higher lands from continuous cropping without manuring, and the scanty crops raised on them, contrasting unfavourably with the crops grown by irrigation on the lower-lying lands, which had probably been uncultivated and covered with jungle, and were freshly broken up, would be another reason for migration to the lower lands.

The higher lands being deserted would go out of cultivation, and the ridges round the fields would not be kept up, as was formerly the case when under cultivation: this would induce greater surface-drainage, and lead to greater damage from that cause.

As irrigation extended, consolidation of the extended area of the irrigated lands would increase and cause further surface-drainage.

As the surface-drainage increased, the less water would remain in the soil, and more would have to be supplied to produce a crop. The more water supplied the harder and more impermeable would the soil become; the greater the impermeability of the soil to water supplied by irrigation the sooner would that water be lost by evaporation, and a further supply of water be required.

When irrigation was limited to what could be done from

wells, the laborious systems of raising the water from them, and the expense, was a pretty safe guarantee of water being but sparingly used. Some canals were dug in Upper India in the times of the Mahommedan emperors, but these do not appear to have been used to irrigate lands under grain crops, or, if so, to a very small extent, and their effect for good or bad on the country generally could hardly have been felt.

This increasing demand for water would lower the spring level, the wells would have to be deepened, the water would have to be raised from a greater depth, entailing greater expense, until at length canals were undertaken to supply water at a cheaper rate than it could be raised from wells; these canals, by furnishing a greater supply of water, have exaggerated the evil, and now, those portions of the country first subjected to canal irrigation are covered with reh and are sterile, and the produce of land more lately brought under the influence of the canals is yearly decreasing.

This evil has been caused by thinking that engineering was agriculture, or could supplant agriculture; that water was the one thing wanted for agriculture, and that water being supplied by engineering works agriculture must succeed,—a grievous mistake, as is evident to every one but the irrigationists—a mistake which has cost an immense amount of money; but governments, as well as individuals, must pay for experience.

If irrigation had been absolutely necessary, and crops could not have been grown without its aid, there could have been no help for it; but when we see the evil results of irrigation, and know that cultivation can be carried on without it, and without injury resulting to the land—nay, further, that the land, under another and more rational system of husbandry, may be yearly improving in quality, the quantity of the produce being steadily increasing till the maximum per acre were reached, it seems unaccountable why the system of irrigation is persisted in.

That irrigation is not necessary in Upper India, is evident from the following facts.

I have stated that, in 1835, according to Government records, only one acre was irrigated to 126 unirrigated, of the cultivated land in the Budaon district. Now the proportion is one acre irrigated to three unirrigated. Three-fourths of the land is cultivated without irrigation. From a return of surveyed and assessed area in the North-Western Provinces for 1868-69, of a total of 24,105,849 acres cultivated, 8,912,235 are returned as irrigated and 11,919,996 as unirrigated, details of irrigated and unirrigated not being given for five districts, the non-irrigated being in excess of the irrigated in the proportion of about 4 to 3.

These non-irrigated lands *do yearly produce crops under a most miserable and wretched system of cultivation.* The crops are poor, but that is owing to bad cultivation; good crops could not be expected under the circumstances; the soil being merely scratched two or three inches deep, the moisture in the soil quickly dries up and the crop is poor. No attempt has been made to teach a better style of agriculture, but irrigation only is recommended to supply water, to replace what has been lost by negligent cultivation.

If, then, under a wretched, defective system of farming, crops can be produced without irrigation, in which system, too, no attempts are made to retain the rainfall in the soil, what may we not expect to effect when we apply a better system, and do our utmost to retain the rainfall in the land?

I have mentioned that the more water is supplied to the land by irrigation the more will the land require.

I was formerly a believer in irrigation. I went to Budaon in 1858, and had a fair-sized garden there; up till 1865 (when

I took leave to England) I found with a pair of bullocks I could keep it sufficiently irrigated, and the three men and a boy I had employed in it could keep it in order. I returned to Budaon in January, 1867, and shortly afterwards found one pair of bullocks could not raise sufficient water, so had to get a second pair. The water in my garden is raised from a well in a large leathern bucket, worked by a rope over a wheel. Three men are engaged in the operation; one to drive the bullocks, one to land the bucket when it arrives at the well's mouth, and one to look after the water channels and to distribute the water to the different beds. Thus three out of my four garden hands were employed in irrigating the garden. One pair of bullocks worked from early in the morning till ten or eleven o'clock, and the other pair in the afternoon; so the time of three men was pretty well taken up in irrigation, and the garden was always out of order and untidy. As the soil got more and more hardened more water had to be given, it being more quickly lost by evaporation. Last year, 1872, at the commencement of the rains, I had one plot dug up some sixteen or eighteen inches deep, the lumps of earth being well broken. I had it sown with jowar (*Holcus sorghum*), and shortly before the end of the rains I had the jowar crop cut down and buried a foot deep in the field. As soon as the rains had finished, about 20th September, I planted potatoes in this piece of ground.

I had just been reading a book of Mr. Holt Beevor's, in which he recommended planting potato-sets nine or ten inches deep in the ground. I followed his advice, although I had never before planted potato-sets more than five or six inches deep. The consequence of deep planting was that not half the sets came up.

On referring to Stephen's "Book of the Farm," I found he said potatoes would not show above ground if planted, I think he said, eight inches deep. I have not his book by me to refer to, but am nearly sure eight inches is what he says. The plants that did come up grew very well, but their tops were killed by frost in December. The tubers, when dug up, though numerous, were small, growth having of course ceased when the tops were killed by frost. The reasons of partial failure are clear: too deep planting of the sets, and want of protection from frost.

In repeating this experiment I should plant the potato-sets only six inches in the ground, and to save the plants from frost, should have a good number of castor-oil or other quick-growing plants sown on the land to check radiation of heat from the soil at night, or prepare land somewhat shaded. We are too apt in India to follow in gardening the directions of English gardeners, and expose plants as much to the sun as possible. Nearly all the vegetables and plants from temperate climates succeed best in India when partially shaded. By planting a few trees in gardens every vegetable can be shaded for an hour or two every day, which is all that is required in the cold weather.

To return to my experiments: the rains ceased about the 20th September. About the end of January (I cannot speak to dates here, not having my journal with me), the rain from 20th September to that time being only four-tenths of an inch, I took some soil from the potato plot from eight inches below the surface. I weighed out several *seers* of the soil and placed them separately exposed to the sun. The thermometer in the sun, when I exposed the earth, stood at 103° Fahrenheit. The several parcels of soil were exposed for two hours; at the end of that time the thermometer stood at 75°, the day being cloudy. I then weighed the several parcels of soil, and in each there was a loss of upwards of two *chittacks*. There are sixteen chittacks to the seer, so the loss was more than one-eighth of the weight, or upwards of 12½ per cent. This soil was at eight inches from the surface; at a few inches lower down the soil was much moister, but I did not test it.

To get rid of all its moisture, a substance must be exposed for a lengthened time to a temperature of 212° Fahr. I had not the necessary apparatus for carrying out the experiment properly, and the soil was not exposed to a greater heat than 103° at any time during the trial.

Another plot in my garden I also had dug up rather late in the rains, sixteen or eighteen inches deep, and sown with jowar. I wanted here to see to what extent the land would be dried by letting the crop stand for some time after the cessation of the rains, so I had the crop cut and buried in the soil of the field one foot deep, about ten days or a fortnight after the rains had ceased. On half this plot I sowed peas in rows, and between the rows, beetroot, radishes, turnips, &c. From the crop of jowar having been allowed to stand after the rains had ceased, the soil had become dry; the water in it had been taken up by the roots and given off from the leaves of the jowar, consequently the seeds of vegetables which I sowed did not germinate, from want of moisture, except in a few shaded places. I irrigated this land once; the ground having been so deeply dug took a great deal of water, but with that one watering the vegetables came to perfection, and never appeared as if they wanted any more water.

The other half of this plot I sowed with linseed—the seed from the former year's crop, which was raised from seed bought in the bazar. This was treated in exactly the same way, and was once irrigated. The crop of flax was as good as any I have seen in England. Flax is sown in India only for its seed, the fibre is not known as an article of any commercial value by the natives, and the plant is used for fuel or thrown away.

Another plot of my garden I had trenched about two feet deep, also early in the rains. I did not, in this case, grow a crop to bury as manure. Shortly after the rains I transplanted into some of this land cauliflowers and cabbages. When brought from the bed where grown and planted out, each plant got about a pint of water, and the same amount of water two days later. Beyond this these plants were not watered. The only rain that fell from the conclusion of the rains till the end of January or commencement of February was only four-tenths of an inch. The cauliflowers did not, as is usually the case with them when irrigated, all flower at once, but lasted for a long time : this might partly be caused by some of the plants being more shaded than others. The great difference, however, was in the flavour; these cauliflowers, grown without irrigation, being infinitely superior to the insipid, watery plants grown by irrigation, and were not inferior in size and weight. I had good opportunities of making comparisons, as in the remainder of my garden I grew vegetables in the usual way with irrigation, and from the same seeds.

The peas I have mentioned as grown being irrigated only once, came into bearing earlier, and continued to bear some time later, than peas of the same kinds the seed from the same packets, sown on the same day, and irrigated; and the flavour of the non-irrigated, or rather once-irrigated, peas was also superior to that of those which had to be irrigated at least once a week to keep them alive.

It was interesting to watch these plants and compare their appearance during growth. The unirrigated plants were throughout more healthy, looked more vigorous, and their leaves of a deeper, darker green than the irrigated plants.

I purposely kept water away from some of the irrigated vegetables for a short time, and the consequence was they soon withered away, the moisture in the ground within reach of their roots being speedily dried up from evaporation, the soil having been but shallowly cultivated.

Having succeeded in cultivating the greater part of my garden without irrigation, I sold one pair of bullocks; the remaining pair had but little to do in the way of raising water. My men were not perpetually at work at the well; they had time to look after the more necessary operations of the garden, and it has been in better order than it used to be in before.

As the vegetables were used I had the ground dug up; the difference that had taken place in the texture of the soils where the jowar crop had been buried was most remarkable. The soil, of the description known as "muttiār," a stiff, clayey soil, sticky when wet, and almost as hard as stone when dry, and which was very hard and difficult to dig and break up in preparation for the jowar, had become quite free-working and friable. I forgot to mention, regarding the plot on which I planted the potatoes, that in the hot weather, previous to digging up the soil, I had burnt some of the surface-soil and spread the ashes over the land. There might have been two cubic yards of ashes spread over between 300 and 400 square yards of land. The whole of the land, which had been green manured, was now in the condition of a light loam, the potato plot which had had the ashes being the easier to work.

Besides these experiments in the garden, I tried a patch of potatoes in a field. The soil here was merely deeply dug. There was no crop buried in it. The sets were planted deeply, at eight or nine inches; many did not come up, but those that did looked very healthy till killed by frost. On digging up the potatoes, the number of tubers to each plant was great, but they were small, the haulm having been killed by frost in December, after which there would be no further growth.

Culinary vegetables require a greater amount of moisture, than cereals; and here I succeeded in growing them without irrigation, as I have described. If these can be grown, why not cereals? The fact is, that people have heard so much about the supposed benefits of irrigation, that they do not seem to be aware that any crop can be grown unless continually swamped with water. I doubt much if the people who so strongly advocate irrigation have tried cultivation on a rational system without it. While on the subject of vegetables, potatoes more particularly, it is worthy of remark, that where these are grown by the natives, in the cold weather, when frost is apprehended, they take care to keep their potato plots well irrigated, thoroughly soaked: they say the water being warm keeps off frost. The fact is that a soil thoroughly soaked with water is a bad radiator of heat, and does not cool down to the extent it would do when drier, consequently crops growing on such a soil are not injured by frost to the extent they would be were the soil drier. There are, however, better and cheaper ways of guarding against frost.

In 1869 I had a piece of land of the description of soil known as "doomat," ploughed with the country plough, about eight or nine inches deep. This land had been cultivated previously under irrigation. I determined to try it without irrigation; but as it looked dry, I irrigated a few small beds on one side of the field in the commencement of March. The crop on the irrigated part became laid, and the irrigation evidently did more harm than good. Perhaps one-twentieth of the field was irrigated. The crop from my field was twelve-fold the amount of seed sown, only a poor crop, but it suffered from want of water; the soil dried up from not having been sufficiently deeply cultivated, and from my only having had it banked up late in the rains, and most of the rain-water having been allowed to run off. Poor as my crop was, the crop on the next field, cultivated by a native in the usual way, was worse. He sowed the same amount of seed on a smaller plot of ground, on the same day that I did, and irrigated his field three times; his crop was only, according to his statement, threefold the seed sown. My crop was at the rate of nearly twenty-three bushels per acre, and his a little over nine bushels.

It is necessary in estimating the value of a crop, to take into consideration the produce per acre, the increase of produce over seed sown, the amount expended in manure, and the cost of the cultivation of the land. I gave my field a dressing of farmyard manure, a few broken bones, and some brick-kiln ashes. The manuring I gave my field would have been considered a very light one in England. I, however, mentioned this case in a pamphlet I published in 1870, and am told that the excess of my crop over that of the next field was due to the "*heavy dressing*" of manure — no inquiries having been made as to the amount of manure used by me. I doubt if the cost of preparing my field and applying manure was as much as in preparing it the usual way, as fewer ploughings were given. No money was expended in irrigation, and the produce was more. That the produce was not still more was owing to the land not being taken in hand early enough in the season, and to its not being ploughed sufficiently deep. Since 1869 I have had a rain crop, and a cold-weather crop, every year from this field without irrigation, and in no single case has the crop raised by me been in any way inferior to the crops on the surrounding fields, although only one crop has been taken each year from them, and in general my crops have been markedly better. Objection was taken to this experiment, as it was on a small scale. As a servant of Government I am precluded from making any large experiments, or should gladly have done so. I cannot, however, admit the argument that what has succeeded on a small scale would fail on a larger scale. The contrary is more likely to be the case. I have on this field purposely avoided cultivating the soil above eight or nine inches deep, as I wished to see if that was sufficiently deep to ensure crops without irrigation. I have raised crops fully equal to my neighbours, besides getting two crops every year when they only got one, still I consider the depth of eight or nine inches insufficient, and that a greater depth would give increased crops.

I have mentioned the amount of unirrigated lands yearly producing crops as a proof that crops can be grown without irrigation, the reason seems to be that the unirrigated lands are lighter and more easily and deeply worked. In the Budaon district a fair amount of sugar-cane is grown on high land which is never irrigated, and the yield is not much, if at all, inferior to that of crops on the irrigated lands.

The land is prepared in the following way :—After a cold-weather crop has been taken from a field in March or April the land remains untouched till the rains, when it is dug with mattocks, the natives say a foot or eighteen inches deep. I doubt their being dug above eight or ten inches deep. Sometimes ridges are made round the field to prevent loss of water by surface-drainage, and allow the rain-water to sink into the soil. Where the land is level, the ridges round the field are sometimes not made, it being considered that deeply loosening the soil will allow sufficient water to penetrate, and will retain it. The land is ploughed occasionally through the following cold weather to thoroughly pulverize the soil, and it is manured. The cane is planted in February or March, which, finding moisture in the deeply-cultivated soil, does not require irrigation. Sometimes sugar-cane is taken after a rain crop without irrigation; in this case the land only has the rain of the cold weather in it to supply the wants of the crop.

The juice of canes from unirrigated land is said to contain a greater percentage of saccharine matter, and to be of a superior quality to that obtained from irrigated land. Here is a plant, planted at the commencement of the hot weather, which grows through the whole of the hot dry weather, simply from the land being deeply cultivated, and its retaining moisture from having been more deeply cultivated and manured. In these unirrigated sugar-cane fields it is usual to sow the seeds of the water-melon and other cucurbitaceous plants which ripen their fruits during the hot weather and in the commencement of the rains. Here is tolerable proof that deep cultivation will retain sufficient moisture in the land for the wants of plants, even in the hottest and driest season of the year.

Sugar-canes and melons, plants requiring a large amount of moisture, sown in March, six months after the end of the rains, at the commencement of the driest time of the year, when there is no perceptible dew, grow during the hot winds, the melons bearing fruit, notwithstanding their being in an isolated field, in an open plain, and surrounded by fields the bare surface of which is in a condition to generate heat. Still it is said that irrigation is necessary for ordinary cereals (wheat and barley) which require less moisture, are sown about a month after the end of the rains, when there are heavy dews during the greater portion of their period of growth, when the greater part of the country is under crops, and absorbs and radiates heat, and does not generate it, and when there is a fair amount of humidity in the air, which would be increased were the land more deeply cultivated.

I have been told there must have been some peculiarity in the soil where sugar-cane and melons were grown without irrigation. The only peculiarity was the soil was more deeply cultivated and manured. I recommended a thakur zemindar to try cultivating sugar-cane on his land, substituting deep cultivation for irrigation. This was in a part of the Budaon district where sugar-cane is always cultivated under irrigation. He tried, and succeeded, and told me his cane was fully as good as any grown in the neighbourhood, and had cost him very much less to produce. This is on stiff soil totally different to the light soils before mentioned. The zemindar further said that he intended to keep to the system of deep cultivation instead of irrigation for sugar-cane, and his neighbours also were going to adopt it, as being more profitable. He paid under 1r. 8a. (less than three shillings) per acre for having his land dug eight inches deep.

I was told in April last, on my way to England on a Peninsular and Oriental steamer, by an officer of high standing in the Bengal Civil Service, who had been employed a good deal in the Dooab, that where heaps of silt had been piled up, taken from the canal in clearing it out, crops of wheat and barley grew on the heaps, without irrigation, so rank that they had to be used as green food for cattle. Here, again, is a proof that soil loosely thrown together will retain sufficient moisture by capillary attraction for the use of cereal crops. The gentleman who gave me this information was formerly a very stanch advocate of irrigation, but had somewhat moderated his views on the subject. The evidence I shall now bring forward as to the power of retaining moisture possessed by deeply-cultivated soils I take from the supplement to *Gazette of India* of 18th January, 1873.

EXTRACT *from the Annual Administration Report of the Cotton Department of the Bombay Presidency for* 1871-72 :—

" The difference, however, in the quantity of water required for irrigating land ploughed deeply by the English, and lightly by the native plough, is, as mentioned by Mr. Strachan, very remarkable. He says, speaking of the English plough, ' The cotton-plants thrive much better on land turned over with it, and also require less water than they do on soil ploughed with the country plough, the yield of cotton per acre on land tilled with English tools being twelve pounds above the highest return of any of our other fields, though land wrought with the foreign implements was *considerably inferior in quality* to the field from which our highest return by the native system of culture was obtained. The former was four times watered, while *the latter got nine waterings all over, and part of it got ten.*'

"Deep ploughing, in addition to its direct advantage to the plant, would thus appear to result in the saving of a considerable amount (say fifty per cent.) of water in irrigation, and consequently, in addition, in a saving of cattle power, and therefore of expense in lifting the water. It may thus, if proved to be as advantageous as would appear, and if largely practised in years to come, eventuate in the saving of large sums of money in irrigation works, and even tend to reduce the disposition to certain classes of fever now said to be so prevalent in the neighbourhood of irrigation canals. Further, it would appear to double the advantage received from a fixed supply. If this be the case, the rainfall in a district where it is naturally scanty and insufficient, would, in effect, be artificially and indirectly *doubled* by this deep ploughing and superior treatment of the soil."

In the same extract, the plough sent by the Marquis of Tweeddale is mentioned as being "very easy to work."

The extract given about the cultivation of cotton refers to experiments made, I believe, in the Province of Scinde, notorious as having the smallest rainfall of any part of India; and here deep cultivation reduces the amount of water required by one-half. In the greater part of Upper India cotton does not require irrigation, as it is sown early in the rains. I have grown it at the rate of upwards of 350 lb. of clean cotton to the acre without irrigation. There is an idea prevalent that Indian cotton is an annual; but this is a mistake. Where allowed to stand, and protected, it will bear the second year, but the pods are small, being dried up by the hot winds. Were the excessive *dry heat* of the hot winds diminished, the plant would doubtless bear well the second year. In exposed cotton-fields, as the plants break into leaf in February and March, all are eaten down by cattle, and the plant has no chance of surviving. Sugar-cane, too, in India, is treated as an annual. In other countries, where there are not such excessively dry seasons, it is allowed to stand for a second or even a third year, the suckers thrown out from the roots giving a second and third crop.

Another proof of the power of loosened surface-soil to prevent the too great loss of moisture, and to retain sufficient in the subsoil for the purposes of vegetation, is furnished by the "Sarkarra" grass. This grass (in appearance like the "Pampas" grass we see in English gardens), which grows ten or fifteen feet high, is often planted round fields on the high land, to check the drifting of the sand. The sand accumulates about the roots of the plants, and the grass, which is cut down in the cold weather, throws out fresh shoots at the commencement of the hot weather, and grows vigorously through the season, from the moisture in the subsoil not being able to rise by capillary attraction through the loose sand on the surface. On the ridges round the irrigated fields where there is a hard soil, it is rare to see this grass. The subsoil is too dry for it.

There might be some reasonable excuse for canals in parts of the country where the annual rainfall is under ten inches, but there irrigation should be made use of to encourage the growth of trees, and thus increase the humidity of the climate, when irrigation for ordinary grain crops would not be necessary. The rage, however, for irrigational canals is such, that it does not appear to be guided by the amount of annual rainfall, and we see canals projected to irrigate parts of the country with an ample rainfall. The Eastern Ganges Canal is intended to irrigate portions of the Bijnore and Moradabad districts.

According to a supplement of the *North-West Provinces Gazette*, dated 15th March, 1873, the rainfall from 1st June, 1872, to 3rd March, 1873, at various points in the Bijnore districts, was as follows:—

Nujeebabad	77·2
Nugeena	54·6
Dhampoor	47·2
Bijnore	38·0
Chandpoor	54·3
	5)271·3
Average	54·26

That irrigation should be considered advisable with such a rainfall, shows that advantage cannot be taken of it, that it is allowed to run to waste, most probably by surface-drainage.

Upper India is essentially an agricultural country, and must from its geographical position depend for food for its population on what it can itself produce. Had a mere fraction of the amount expended on irrigational works been spent in improving the agriculture of the country, there would not now have been the increased demand for further engineering works to supply water. But no attempt is made, not a rupee is spent in improving the agriculture of the country, and it is carried on in the old antiquated way. This arises from a want of agricultural knowledge amongst Government officials in India. Agriculture is not included in the various branches of knowledge in which a civilian or a military man has to pass an examination; it is never studied by candidates for Government employ in India; and consequently it is rare to find any Government official in India who has any knowledge of either the theory or practice of agriculture. Engineering is considered agriculture. The cost of canals for irrigation is budgeted under the head of agricultural works, while the truth is canals and irrigation are doing more than anything else to destroy the agricultural prosperity of the country, and to reduce land formerly fruitful to a state of sterility.

Statements periodically appear in the various Government Gazettes showing the amount of land irrigated during the week or fortnight, and the amount of water supplied; the acreage under the various descriptions of crops is carefully laid down, but no statement is published showing the extent of land rendered sterile by reh, or otherwise depreciated by the effects of irrigation. The supposed benefits are made the most of, and the losses are not shown. A rather one-sided way of keeping accounts, and calculated to mislead.

Improvements are being made in every direction, except in agriculture, on which the country is dependent for its very existence. Education is being pushed on, money can be found for that, but as far as I am aware, as much as a five-pound note has not been spent in agricultural education in Upper India in the last twenty-five years. The very branch of knowledge which is most necessary is neglected, the remark met with when suggesting improvements in agriculture being, depend upon it, the natives of a country are the best judges of the style of agriculture adapted to its requirements. I continually had this remark made to me five-and-twenty years ago, and hear the same even now. It seems to be forgotten that the natives of Upper India have had no opportunity of judging, not having seen any other system than that handed down to them from their ancestors. If this argument holds good when applied to the agriculture of a country, why not when applied to all the other requirements of the country,—its engineering and education for instance? But if the old systems of agriculture were to be carried on in every country as handed down from antiquity, all improvement would cease. To be consistent, and to carry the system out in other branches of knowledge, would be simply to ignore all progress and invention. But the system of irrigation is new and has been forced on the country. In Rohilcund it was almost unknown fifty years ago.

Probably irrigation from wells in the Dooab, whence it appears to have spread into Rohilcund, was the result of the supposed benefits of irrigation being continually impressed on the natives by European officials, servants of Government, who possessed no real knowledge of agriculture. There was an excuse for them, their education did not include agriculture, and they knew no better; they thought irrigation the one thing required, and there was not at that time any evidence of its ill effects. In those days, in England, breaking up the pan was considered injurious; it is only lately that the benefits of deeper cultivation of the soil have been fully understood.

It was said that by breaking up the pan useless barren soil was brought to the surface. Mr. Wren-Hoskyns, however, has since then, in his book "Talpa, or Chronicles of a Clay Farm," shown how the worst-looking soils, apparently barren clays, by exposure to the air become fertile; and it is now generally acknowledged that nearly all subsoils, however bad they may appear, are rendered productive by exposure to the air. The irrigationists say that the surface-soil only is productive, the subsoil is bad; if such were the case, which I deny, there would be still greater reason for preventing the surface-soil being washed away, and it would be another argument against surface-drainage. Now the ploughed arable surface-soil is washed away from the higher lands, as the surface of a convex macadamized street, ground to dust by the action of wheels, is washed into the gutters by a heavy shower.

Now that the evils of irrigation are apparent throughout the country, there seems to be no reason for persistence in it.

Agriculture is a continually advancing science. The system suited for a new rich soil, as freshly broken-up jungle or forest land, is not adapted for land that has been for ages under cultivation. The soil of freshly broken-up forest land is chiefly composed of decayed vegetable matter, it requires no manure, and any scratching of the surface will enable it to carry crops. Because this was the case with every field when first broken up and brought into cultivation, this system is forsooth to be continued. We are to ignore the fact that the land has been reduced in fertility by the crops taken from it, that it has been impoverished by mismanagement arising from ignorance, that the vegetable soil which attracted water from the atmosphere and held it has disappeared, and we have in its place a mineral soil which has not the same power of abstracting water from the air and retaining it; the physical condition of the soil has been changed, yet no change is to be made in the manner of its treatment, because that was sufficient in former times, under, however, very different circumstances. The same system being now pursued in an impoverished state of the land, as formerly, when the land was highly fertile, leads to diminished results, which are comparatively retrogressive.

The proportion of produce to seed sown is steadily diminishing, and probably the average produce of lands that are unirrigated, or have been irrigated from canals for ten years, does not exceed fivefold the seed sown.

The reason of the backward state of agriculture in Upper India is plain. No literate natives take to farming as a profession. Nearly all the zemindars, many of them literate men, retain some land in their own hands; but it is merely as a convenience—they do not farm for a livelihood. There are no literate tenants. If a man of the ryot or tenant class becomes proficient in reading and writing, he thinks farming *infra dig.*, and tries to get some appointment where reading and writing are all that is wanted, or where less physical exertion is required than in the prosecution of agricultural operations. The educated natives of Upper India look to reading and writing for a livelihood. Numbers study with the hope of getting an appointment, with some steady emoluments, in which they may pass their lives. Caste prejudices have given way in many cases, as notably in the cases of Hindoos of high caste, who have studied medicine and surgery. These men have studied anatomy and practised dissection, which is repulsive to Hindoo ideas, with the view of qualifying as native doctors and earning a livelihood. There is no caste prejudice against agriculture, all castes engage in it; but those who subsist by agriculture are the poorest of the classes to which they belong. A ten-acre farm held by one person would be considered in many parts of Upper India a large holding. Several members of a family or several friends will conjointly take a greater breadth of land, but the land is generally let in very small holdings. There are no tenants of any decent status in society or of considerable means engaged in farming. The educated natives do not engage in agriculture because they do not see how a livelihood is to be made by it; they do not see any person of a decent status in society living by the profits of farming, and do not understand how it can be done. Were they shown that a respectable livelihood could be gained by farming, numbers of the more respectable classes, more especially the country residents, would engage in it. They can only learn how farming can be profitably carried on by the establishment of farms, attached to which should be schools of agriculture, where the theory and practice of agriculture should be thoroughly demonstrated, or by the encouragement of European colonization in India.

There are numbers of Europeans engaged in tea and coffee cultivation and the manufacture of indigo in India, and there seems to be no valid reason why Europeans should not be able equally well, if not better, to look after a farm with a more varied produce. The men engaged in tea and coffee-growing and in making indigo have all their eggs in one basket. Should anything occur to cause a reduced produce, or should the state of the market be unsatisfactory for the article they are engaged in producing, they have nothing else to fall back on.

The case is different in farming, the products are so various, particularly in India and hot countries where different crops can be grown at different seasons, that should the prices of any one species of produce be unfavourable, the loss on that would be compensated by extra gain on the others. Money laid out in farms and schools of agriculture would be directly reproductive, leaving out of consideration the immense benefit that would accrue indirectly to the country generally from their establishment, which, however, should be the grand object of their existence.

The chief subjects to be taught should be retention of the

rain-water by banking the fields, and deep cultivation, and the use of manures, more particularly green manuring. With these alone the produce of grain-food for man could be raised from about fivefold the amount of seed, which perhaps it now is, to from twenty to fifty or even one hundredfold, which would be amply remunerative. The next object after growing food for the population should be forage crops, or food for cattle, and commercial requirements; these being introduced and grown in rotation with cereals, would increase the crops of the latter.

The soil of a great part of Upper India is a deep alluvial deposit, and merely requires the addition of vegetable matter to make it a most fertile loam. With proper cultivation as good crops could be raised in Upper India as in any part of the world, and it is only the backward state of agricultural knowledge that prevents its being one of the chief granaries of the world.

With the barren, unculturable lands planted with trees, and the unirrigated cultivated lands deeply cultivated, the soil being kept open by judicious manuring, a great improvement in the climate must follow. The temperature of April, May, and June, now the season of the hot winds, would be greatly reduced, and probably the greatest heat we should experience in those months would never exceed 100° Fahr. in the shade, and that only for a couple of hours in the day, while the nights, mornings, and evenings would be cool and pleasant. That 100° Fahr. would be the maximum heat in the shade during the hottest season of the year may, I think, be fairly inferred from the study of the climate of other countries, and a consideration of the causes which increase or diminish the temperature of a country. In Bengal, away from the influence of the action of the sea on temperature, we find it is never necessary to keep the glass doors and windows of houses shut to exclude the heat, the temperature seldom rising above 95°; whereas in Upper India at 6 or 8 degrees further north, and from 400 to 1,000 feet above the sea-level, the doors, &c., of houses have to be closed during the hot weather, from 8 or 9 a.m. till sunset every day, and sometimes have to be kept shut all night for that purpose. This is owing to the state of the surface of the country, and its action on the temperature, *which can be altered.*

At the same time and in the same way that the temperaof the hot weather is reduced, the temperature of the rains would probably be reduced some 10 degrees; and if we are to be guided by the action of forests in equalizing temperature in other countries (reducing the extreme heat of summer and modifying the cold of winter), we may infer that the injurious effects of the frosts of the cold weather might be less.

With the hot-weather temperature reduced and the climate moderated by the methods I have suggested, improvement will take place in all the agricultural produce of the country. If we take wheat as an example, we find that the wheat produced in Upper India has a shrivelled shrunken appearance, and is not the plump grain we find in countries with a moister climate. The shrivelled state of the grain is more marked when the wind sets in steadily from the west, before the crops are ripe; and this early setting in of the west wind is dreaded by the cultivators, as it greatly reduces the weight of the crop. The grain is dried up by the hot dry air before it has time to swell properly, as it would under more favourable conditions, *i.e.* with a more genial and less arid state of the atmosphere. With the temperature of the hot weather reduced, numbers of food-producing plants might be introduced into and flourish in the plains of Upper India, as, for instance, the Spanish chestnut, also many fruit-trees, and the cultivation of the tea-plant might be possible throughout the country.

Silk, too, might be a staple product; the only hindrance to its production now being that the worms are dried up, baked to death, by the dry heat of the hot weather.

Under the system I have sketched out of improving the climate by planting and proper cultivation of the soil, I believe there would be no fear of a scarcity of rainfall or famine. A scanty rainfall in any one year would not so injuriously affect the country, as the amount of moisture held in the soil by capillary attraction from the preceding year would be available for the support of crops; and with it in reserve a very small rainfall would suffice. The longer the system had been pursued the less chance would there be of a scanty rainfall, and the less would it be felt when it did occur. With a flourishing state of agriculture we should hear no more of famines, commercial stagnation, floods ravaging the country, or of any of the evils which are now the results of irrigation and surface-drainage.

ADDENDUM.

Another result of the desiccation of the country from the destruction of forests is the increased damage done by locusts, flights of which are more numerous now than they formerly were. Marsh, in "Man and Nature," says: "The insects most injurious to rural industry do not multiply in or near woods. The locust, which ravages the east with its voracious armies, is bred in vast open plains, which admit the full heat of the sun to hasten the hatching of the eggs, gather no moisture to destroy them, and harbour no birds to feed upon the larvæ." And again he says: "It is only since the felling of the forests of Asia Minor and Cyrene that the locust has become so fearfully destructive in those countries.

In Upper India we find locusts feed by preference on the tops of the highest trees; where, however, there are different kinds of trees of equal height, there are some which they prefer. Where the country is well wooded, locusts almost confine their ravages to the trees, and hardly touch the crops, and there is not that damage done to the crops that there is in a part of the country devoid of trees. This fact furnishes another reason for planting trees in the uncultivated lands throughout the country.

APPENDICES.

A (page 13).

Mrs. Somerville, in her book, "Connexion of the Physical Sciences," says, pp. 284–285, "On land the temperature depends upon the nature of the soil and its products, its habitual moisture or dryness;" and, after describing the effects of the Sahara in raising the temperature, says: "On the contrary, vegetation cools the air by evaporation, and the apparent radiation of cold from the leaves of plants, because they absorb more caloric than they give out;" and again says: "Forests cool the air also, by shading the ground from the rays of the sun, and by evaporation from the boughs." On page 233 we have: "The radiating power of a surface is inversely as its reflecting power, and bodies that are most impermeable to heat, radiate least;" and on page 243: "When radiant heat falls upon a surface, part of it is reflected, and part of it is absorbed; consequently, the best reflectors possess the least absorbing powers."

B (page 51).

Some better method of disposal of town filth should be adopted than polluting rivers with it. Let it be applied to fields surrounded by ridges from which there is no escape by surface-drainage, so that it cannot fall into the rivers, and let the amount applied to the land be not in excess of what crops grown on the land can assimilate, and all will be well. In India, the high price of fuel increases river-pollution. The

Hindoos, finding fuel expensive for cremation, dispose of more of their dead by throwing them into the rivers.

C (page 54).

On the occasion of the reading of a paper by W. Taylor, Esq., "On Famines in India, their Remedy and Prevention," at the room of the Society of Arts, on 18th December, 1873, it was stated in the discussion that followed the reading of the paper, that on the 15th August last the floods were higher than usual over a great part of the country which two months later was, and now is, threatened with famine from drought. This shows how quickly the water ran off and was lost, and the land became dried up.

D (page 66).

Captain Thomason, R.E., an officer of great experience, who has been employed for years on irrigational canals, thus writes of reh:—"In the interests of irrigation, can there be a more important question to settle than the treatment of the 'reh' lands, extending year by year throughout our irrigated districts, and rendering our irrigation worse than useless?" In a note to the above paragraph he says, "Vide Mr. Sherer's report on the Western Jumna Canal districts, submitted to Government in 1856-57, and many other reports;" and adds: "From personal observation I can testify to the rapid extension of 'reh' land in the Bareilly district, from 1863 to 1868."

Captain Thomason recommended subsoil-drainage and deep cultivation as a remedy. The drainage where tiles were used, cost, according to his estimate, 20 Rs. or £2 per acre. 50,000 square miles are, according to "Forecast of Expenditure on Canals" (mentioned on page 73), to be secured from liability to drought by irrigation-works, at an expenditure of some £20,000,000. If by this it is meant that an area of 50,000 square miles, or 32,000,000 acres, is to be irrigated at the above cost, then the cost of irrigational works is, in the first case, 12s. 6d. per acre; but as irrigation produces "reh" on the surface of the land, it is suggested an expenditure of £2 per acre be incurred to get rid of the reh. A certain sum having been spent in endeavours to improve the land, which endeavours, instead of improving, have caused deterioration, it is proposed to expend more than three times the original sum in endeavours to mitigate the injurious effects of the first injudicious expenditure. Leaving aside the question of expense, where could the fuel be found to burn the tiles? Supposing subsoil-drainage were carried out, and the reh were carried away by the drains, would this be beneficial or hurtful to the country? It is generally admitted that reh rises by capillary attraction from the subsoil in a state of solution. Such being the case—and I believe it is not disputed, the lands now covered with reh, and sterile from its effects, must have held the reh (except such as may have been brought in the water used for irrigation) in the subsoil at the time they were fertile and bearing good crops, viz. the first few years after they were irrigated; thus showing that land containing the salts composing "reh" in the subsoil, are not sterile but fertile. Getting rid of the reh by the drains might be the means of securing good crops for a few years; but as the salts composing *reh* are in moderate quantities absolutely necessary for vegetation, we might be securing a temporary benefit at the cost of a permanent loss to the country. We might benefit the present generation by ruining posterity.

Many people look on lands once covered with reh as irreclaimably barren. I do not take such a pessimist view of the case; I look on reh as a safeguard thrown up by nature to protect herself from further spoliation, and as a warning to man not to violate her laws; and I believe that by judicious management and giving up irrigation, the reh-covered lands may be made to produce double or quadruple the crops *they ever did with irrigation*. Proper management is all that is required. We must undo all that has been done by irrigation to these lands, and commence a new system. By deep cultivation and manuring we must keep the soil loose and open, and thus we shall prevent water and the salts in solution rising to the surface by capillary attraction, and at the same time, by preventing loss of rain-water by evaporation, we shall encourage the downward filtration of the water, and replenish the deeper springs, and the salts will remain diffused in the soil at a sufficient depth from the surface to supply the wants of plants for ages, and still not be in such excess in the upper soil as to be injurious. A few experiments carefully carried out would prove the correctness or otherwise of the system I advocate, and their cost would be trifling.

Rain-water has two duties to perform,—to furnish moisture for crops, and to replenish the deep-seated springs. Where drainage, either surface or subsoil, is carried out throughout a country, the springs must suffer, and the water-supply will be deficient in dry seasons.

THE END.

www.ingramcontent.com/pod-product-compliance
Lightning Source LLC
Chambersburg PA
CBHW020149170426
43199CB00010B/948